ADVANCE PRAISE FOR
A Woman's Voice Should Be Heard

"I find that a woman's path through life always tells a unique story that needs to be told or read. Aggie's story is nostalgic, thought-provoking, and most of all inspiring to women of all ages. Finding your voice in life can be a poetic and memorable moment. Aggie's found hers in a time when women were first recognizing their pathway to social and economic equality. Aggie's voice helped define the free-thinking, determined women we see as business leaders, educators, and community servants of today."

—**KERRY MISCAVAGE,** Times Leader Media Group Publisher, Wilkes-Barre, PA

"Aggie Jordan's memoir reminds us that we women must not hesitate to speak out when our voices are ignored. The battle for women's equality continues as seen by the recent rejection of *Roe vs. Wade* by the Supreme Court. Aggie's stories of her Irish Catholic family, her life in the convent, the importance of women mentors in her life, and her struggles with corporations and the Small Business Administration demonstrate the courage it takes for women to continue the battle for equality."

—**JUDY MANDEL**, Author *New York Times* bestseller *Replacement Child* and *White Flag*

"Dedication and determination are the key ingredients in this significant memoir by Aggie Jordan. A must-read for anyone intrigued to learn how a successful Catholic nun decides to leave the convent, marry, raise a family and build a prosperous business with 500 employees! The struggle for women's rights is made up of millions of individual stories. Aggie Jordan's story is a reminder to all of us that determination and commitment are required to build a world that improves women's rights."

—**MARIE McKEE**, SVP, Corning Incorporated, (Retired)

"Courage, conviction, and chutzpah are among the strengths that Dr. Jordan drew upon as she fought for recognition and visibility for herself and other women in a male-dominated culture. Gifted with an energy and enthusiasm that few exhibit or can sustain, she rejected the limited roles that so many women believed were their only choices. Today in a culture where misogynist males are still struggling in a world they can't relate to, every woman needs to read about what one strong voice can accomplish."

—**MAUREEN C. WHITE**, Executive Assistant to the President (Retired) State University of New York at Binghamton

"Aggie's memoir will keep your interest word after word."

— **ANITA PUGLISI**, VP of Video Production, The Walt Disney Company

A WOMAN'S VOICE SHOULD BE HEARD

MY JOURNEY FROM THE CONVENT TO THE BATTLE FOR WOMEN'S EQUALITY

AGGIE JORDAN, Ph.D.

A Woman's Voice Should be Heard
My Journey from the Convent to the Battle for Women's Equality

by Aggie Jordan, Ph.D.

Copyright ©2022 by Aggie Jordan, Ph.D.

Published by Legacy Book Press
www. legacybookpress.com

Cover and book design: BookSavvyStudio.com
Cover photos: Ming Louie

Library of Congress Control Number: 111637566595

ISBN: 979-8-9867874-1-1 (paperback)
ISBN: 979-8-9867874-2-8 (hardcover)

Printed in the United States of America

This book is dedicated to Robert DeLaurenti, my husband and my best friend. He has been the witness to my life for the last 48 years. He has supported my voice, encouraging me to make sure it is heard and to follow it with action. He has trusted me with his children as they became our children: Mary DeLaurenti, Gina Napoli, Robert DeLaurenti II, and Michelle Nichols, to whom I also dedicate this book.

It has been a glorious and fulfilling life that they have given me.

Contents

Preface

THE STRUGGLE FOR WOMEN'S EQUALITY GOES ON. The last three decades of the 20th century witnessed major accomplishments for women. State laws were passed to allow married women to own property (Texas, 1965). The law now requires married businesswomen to be treated equally by financial institutions according to the Fair Banking Act (1974). Women became more readily accepted in medical schools and law schools. Girls began to believe that they could choose to be anything they wanted to be: mothers or not, single or married, astronauts, chief executive officers, judges, television anchors or sports broadcasters, basketball or golf professionals, or tennis stars. More women now go to college and universities than their male colleagues. The United States Supreme Court in 1973 recognized a woman's right over her own body in *Roe vs. Wade*. We have made great progress, but all battles have not been won. Recently (June 2022), the US Supreme Court rejected *Roe vs. Wade*.

The Equal Rights Amendment failed to pass the required 38 states to become a constitutional amendment. The Supreme Court at 5-4 voted to take away a woman's right if and when she should give birth through their rejection of her right to an abortion. On that court are six conservative Roman Catholic justices, four of whom voted for rejecting *Roe vs. Wade:* Alito, Barrett, Kavanaugh, and Thomas. The fifth vote, Justice Gorsuch, is an Episcopalian.

There is no doubt that this fight for women's rights has been a religious battle. Catholics, Christian fundamentalists, Baptists, and conservative politicians have joined forces to take away a woman's right to privacy. According to the latest poll of *ABC News* and *The*

Washington Post (November 2021), three out of four respondents believe that a woman's choice for an abortion should be between only her and her doctor.

Recently a dear friend sent me a tee shirt with the following message, "I AM WOMAN, I AM INVINCIBLE, I AM TIRED." Yes, I have fought the battles, as has my friend and so many other women, and we thought we had made sufficient progress for the movement to carry on. How wrong we were. We cannot afford to be tired. We must encourage the young women to take up the cause, and we must support them.

I am not a conservative Catholic. I welcomed Pope John XXIII's invitation to open the Church's windows and let the wind blow through. I felt one with him when he encouraged me to examine my faith and honor my womanhood by participating actively in the church. Yet, I and all women are still restricted. Women cannot be priests in the Catholic Church. Pope John XXIII was hardly in the grave when his successor, Paul VI, decided to slam those windows shut and lock them tight. Women rebelled by simply ignoring Paul's and his bishops' ultimatum. They would practice birth control, take the pill, or get an IUD. They would do whatever it takes to defend their own bodies, limit their families if they so choose and, within their circumstances, abort when necessary.

I am not a lawyer so I will leave the law to the experts. But I am a Catholic, a liberal one who believes in Jesus, in the ancient Church he founded based on loving our neighbor. I'm not sure the institutionalized Catholic Church is the same as when Jesus called his disciples "to come follow me." I believe in my right to choose what I believe makes sense. I was a nun for 14 years, and I believed in serving the Church and her people. Women are her people. I want all her people to be respected and honored for their own beliefs and how they influence the reality of their lives. I believe that those Catholics on the Supreme Court are wrong. They have interlaced their politics and their religion, plus they have used their authority to set women upon a "straight and narrow" path as these justices see it.

The battle for a woman's right to choose what is good and sacred for her own body is not the only battle going on today. Many women endure unjust treatment in their jobs and careers. The "Me Too" movement has demonstrated how men of power have gotten away with sexual and physical abuse. But I am hopeful that women will continue to fight. They want their voices to be heard and their echoes to resound down through the centuries. This takes leadership, a willingness to support your sisters, and a focused attention on what is happening to young girls.

This book, *A Woman's Voice Should Be Heard: My Journey from the Convent to the Battle for Women's Equality*, is definitely a story of a female protagonist. It examines my experiences as an Irish Catholic girl. I grew up in a small town, West Pittston, Pennsylvania, with an uncle who was a priest and a grandmother, mother, and aunt with their strong influence (plus all their biases) on who I became – a Catholic nun for 14 years. The 12 years of Catholic schooling undoubtedly contributed to that decision, and those background stories shine light on why a young girl joins the convent. But why did she stay and then leave?

Other stories describe what the novitiate training of a girl of 17 was like. I describe my eight years of teaching and the challenges I faced living in a convent with 15 other very human females whose passions ran the gamut of society. My love of the students combined with my joy in teaching, and my understanding that I received a calling from God to serve him, allowed me to be happy in a very enclosed structure, a cocoon. And then metamorphosis – an assignment to study at the University of Notre Dame for a master's degree. The pupal stage came to its end.

The environment of Notre Dame in the late 1960s, like so many American universities, was ripe for change. Living in a dorm with brilliant women, all recognizing what was happening with the women's movement, gave me the courage to question my lack of friends in my community; my vows of poverty, chastity, and obedience; and the basic tenets of what I believed was God's new call.

Graduate school for so many reasons was the crucible for my future. I finally became an adult responsible for my own life. And I became a feminist. With a Ph.D. in higher education administration, this feminist found herself as a dean at a university fighting to be heard among a nearly all-male administration. After I left the convent, a new job at General Motors Institute strengthened my voice with the support of a few women colleagues. But my personal life needed work. With the support of a woman friend, I learned to set personal goals. Her encouragement opened the door for me to meet and marry my husband and to start a business.

My initial focus in my business was to train women and managers to work together so that the women could become viable and successful company employees. In the meantime, I had to learn to speak out for my own rights as a woman business owner. The stories are multitudinous, but there are three where the effective results flowed from major combats: a lawsuit against the Small Business Administration; a confrontation with a bank that insisted on my husband's signature so I could obtain loans; and a battle against 250 corporate officers who ejected women business owners from the Minority Business Development Council in Dallas, a membership that women had held for years. Success came because women gathered together, supported one another, and had their voices heard.

These battles created changes that fashioned an America where women could succeed. But the confrontation for women's rights goes on. My hope is that the stories of my life will inspire other women to let their voices be heard when they are engaged in their own struggles. When women support each other, they gain confidence to have their voices heard.

It is with this intention that I write. May the women readers be inspired to find their own voices.

As with all memoirs, this book is based on my memories and my records. I respect those who have their own memories of what may have happened in the situations described. This is my story of how I, a product of a strong Irish Catholic upbringing and 12 years of Catholic school, chose to become a nun and to teach in Catholic schools. It is also the story of my turning point in graduate school at the University of Notre Dame where religion and feminism met each other.

Strong women in my life encouraged me to be heard. And there were strong women in authority who fought me and their own feminism. It is a story of success but not without the battles to be engaged, the sorrows to be endured, and the prices to be paid. I got fired from General Motors, but I was hired in the aerospace industry. I had set a goal to get married within a year when there was no man in my life. That bold, successful plan gave me the courage to step up when the fight for women's equality called.

You will see that the stories I tell here of these battles made the struggles worth it. They created change that made this world a better place for women. I hope you enjoy your read. If you do, or if you don't, please feel free to contact me at info@aggiejordan.com. I love discussions.

May your voice be heard.

PART ONE

The Early
Influence of
Strong Women

CHAPTER ONE

A Girl's Voice Should Be Heard

"**S**HE'S GOT A MOUTH ON HER," I overheard my Grandma Nana say to her daughter, my Aunt Mary. She evidently heard my three-year-old grumble. I was having difficulty locating a towel Auntie sent me to fetch for her.

Undoubtedly I had my hands on my hips as I approached the kitchen doorway and cried out to my aunt, "I can't find it. You come look,"

"You're a bold one, now, aren't ya, little one," Nana said as she pointed her witch-like finger at me.

Nana's Irish brogue was as scary to me as that shaking finger. Bold was a new word for me, and I knew she did not mean "good." I gave her a look of disgust, shook my dark straight hair at her, and stomped out the kitchen door. My bad feelings about Nana, then and forever after, were colored by that very early encounter.

NANA GRANAHAN

My Nana immigrated from Ireland when she was 14 but, at 74, she gave us the impression that children should be ignored; seen and not heard — something I as a child disagreed with. But the treatment we got as children did not always match up with the modeling that the women in my family demonstrated, especially Nana.

As young Maura, Nana came alone to America at that young age with determination. Today I admire her boldness, her courage to break away from her father, brothers, and sister to make that arduous trip across the ocean. Her mother died in childbirth with her fifth child. Her father, Willie Clarke, had remarried within 90 days of her mother's death. When he brought a strange woman into the home to replace her mother during this time of grief, the teenage Maura cried for weeks. She could not tolerate her mother being replaced by another woman. She begged her father to let her emigrate to America. Her mother's sister, Aunt Kate, was in northeastern Pennsylvania. Through many letters, Aunt Kate begged her brother-in-law, Willie, to send his daughter to her.

When I visited Ireland, I found the death certificate that indicated Nana's mother died of fever at the age of 38. The certificate indicated that "the husband reported that after childbirth, Ellen Jackson Clarke had the fever for 30 days with no medical attention." Did my great-grandfather, Willie, let his wife die without helping her? Did he have an affair with this woman that he married so quickly? I relayed the story to my mother and asked her, "Do you think he just left your mom's mom to die —he didn't get her any medical help?" My mother didn't hesitate.

"He could have. My mother felt her father abandoned her when he married that woman. She felt he had betrayed her mother, and she never forgave him."

My relatives in Ireland had a kinder view. They believed that Nana's father, our great-grandfather Willie Clarke, a farmer, had to have help with his five young children. They grew up admiring the woman who raised their own grandfather with much love. They believed the farmer could not do it alone, and so remarrying quickly was not unusual.

As young Maura, Nana's grief and her unhappiness with the new stepmother cried out for relief. She begged, pleaded, and implored her father every day. She couldn't stop crying. She missed her mother and couldn't tolerate this woman in her house. Finally, the pleading worked. Her father agreed to send her to America but not to her aunt. For some unknown reason, we suspect some family "troubles" as they say in Ireland, he arranged passage to Baltimore to some relatives on his side of the family. Nana never lost her determination to join her aunt. At least she was in America. Working as a scrub maid for four years in a convent, she eventually saved enough money to head north to her Aunt Kate in the anthracite coal region of northeastern Pennsylvania.

Eventually, Nana met and married Papa (John Granahan) and gave birth to ten children. Nana's brother, Patrick, also joined her, and he met and married Annie, Papa's sister. Eventually the whole Granahan and Clarke family moved to a small compound in the Pittston Junction. The Junction was developed by the coal companies, and most of the houses were constructed by them. It became a transit station for the coal freight and eventually was owned by the Lehigh Valley railroad. John and Patrick both worked on the railroad, so it was natural to settle in this area with railroad tracks and freight cars lined up in all directions. My mother and Aunt Mary grew up in this compound of Irish Catholic culture with plenty of women to guide them.

They were a proud Irish clan from Counties Mayo and Sligo who took great satisfaction in their American lives. I don't ever remember humility being honored as a virtue in our family, though outright bragging was unacceptable. But there was no doubt that education, discipline, and religion were deeply held values.

Since I was only four years old when my Nana died, I did not personally experience her powerful history, but I believe I am a product of it. The relatives she left behind made sure we all knew what a strong woman she was: a woman of determination who had a financial talent and who made a successful life. During her marriage, Nana took whatever money was not needed for essentials and invested it in the stock market.

My mother often told us, "Your Nana would get on the Lehigh Valley train in Pittston with one of us in tow and ride to Wilkes-Barre, just to watch the ticker tape on the stock exchange."

Nana would wear a mid-length beige print dress, a brown hat, and caramel gloves standing straight in her 5' 6" frame, staring up at the tape as it traveled across the high border of the train station wall. Through her initial investments in the late 1920s, she made enough money to build her family a home, the same home where I, that three-year-old, stood her ground against this strong woman.

"In 1929, before the crash," my mother bragged, "when everyone else lost money in the stock market, Nana made enough money to buy a new car, the first one in the neighborhood."

The Catholic Church was Nana's rule. Whatever the priest said was God's word, and what happened to anyone in her world (good or bad) was God's will. This faith helped Nana through much grief in her life. Of her ten children, two of them died as adults from tuberculosis, and three did not live past the toddler stage. One died at the age of four when she ran under a pot of scalding hot water that her oldest sister was carrying. Nana rose beyond her loss to comfort her daughter, who never seemed to forgive herself for her part in the accident.

In January of 1930, Papa John died of infection. Nana and Papa's middle son, Leo, was studying for the priesthood and was to be ordained in the spring of 1930. Nana insisted on celebrating this ordination, even during her grief of losing her husband quite unexpectedly a few months earlier.

When Nana died, her body was laid out in the coffin of the family living room. It was the Irish custom to kiss the dead before the burial. My mother thought that Maureen, who was barely two, and I just four should give my Nana a goodbye kiss as she laid in that casket. I resisted kicking and screaming, "No, no. I don't want to." When Maureen heard me cry, tears started falling down her face. Soon my father came to our rescue, picking up both Maureen and me and carrying us off. Perhaps the term "corpse house" is not familiar to you, but that was the term used for wakes at home where I grew up. To this day, I shiver at the term and even fret about going to funeral parlors where bodies are laid out in a casket.

Was Nana's faith the only source of her fortitude? I suppose her upbraiding me for my "speaking out" was an example of her sternness, her firm belief that a three-year-old must respect her elders and behave. This sternness and the "stiff upper lip" were present in my mother as well as her three brothers and, to a lesser degree, in my Aunt Mary.

CHAPTER TWO

My Mother's Voice

M Y MOTHER, AGNES GRANAHAN JORDAN, inherited her mother's mental fortitude as well as the stern discipline that Nana felt necessary in raising children. Growing up in that Irish neighborhood, my mother learned the value of discipline, hard work, education, and the Catholic Church. There were rules. Yes, my mother had a voice to be heard by all of us children and often by the nuns and priests.

I have found that family interaction of praise and hurt, whether at the dining table or watching television together in the living room, has an enormous influence on who we become. For as long as I can remember, I reacted very strongly to anyone, adult or peer, who insinuated that I—or anyone of my three sisters or girlfriends—couldn't do anything, especially speak up.

My brother, JoeJoe, often teased us girls with misogynist banter when we were playing in our backyard. Sometimes he would do it just to get a rise out of me, which he always did. "You're only a girl. You may think you're smart and you'll be somebody, but you won't."

One day, JoeJoe and I scampered over the railroad bridge that crossed the Susquehanna River from West Pittston to go to my aunt's house in the Pittston Junction. The path along the track was very narrow and rocky. The thrill for an 11- and a 14-year-old was escaping the trains that could have been coming. This dangerous feat was forbidden — but it cut off about a mile of the trip, and it was very exciting. Who got the serious scolding from Mother because it was too dangerous for a girl? Me, of course. JoeJoe bullied me for confessing that we took that route when Mother questioned me. "Girls just can't keep secrets," he shouted as he disappeared outside.

On the other hand, when I was 14 and a high school student, I sensed that my brother Leo, six years older than I, respected me. He did not hesitate to get help from me with his college algebra. When he offered to pay me, I knew I had some worth. From then on, I recognized that I enjoyed working for money. He worked at a relative's tire store to earn his way through college. So when he paid me a quarter to press his trousers or to iron his shirts, I knew I would get paid if I accepted the request. We would negotiate the price of each item. In the beginning I would do jobs for him for a dime. Eventually, I learned he was willing to pay more if I held out.

Mother insisted that we earn our keep. We had chores to do because she let us know that, "You eat our food, we buy your clothes, and there's this roof over your head." But Mother often gave conflicting messages about her view of women. She insisted that the girls do the housework and that the boys do the outside work. Yet she encouraged us girls to be good students and insisted that we would go to college. "You're just as good as your brothers. No reason you can't go to college."

Mother finished high school and a year of secretarial training. Her siblings were all college graduates — her sisters became teachers, and her brothers earned professional degrees. Dad only had a tenth-grade education, but he proudly pulled out his report cards and pointed to all his A's with the challenge, "Now see if you can match that." My parents didn't attend college, but from both their lips we heard, "You are going to college." I asked Mother when I was in high school why she didn't want to go to college. She responded, "I didn't want to be a teacher or a nurse, so being a secretary was my only choice."

I questioned whether Mother resented not going to college because she continued to remind us four girls, "You are going to college unless you want to depend on some man to support you." That message was loud, clear, and often. I felt she wasn't very happy with her role as a housewife and mother. She complained a lot about "you kids." Granted, raising seven kids was a morning-to-night job and something I knew

I would never do. I knew she did it out of duty and her unrelenting adherence to the Catholic Church's rules.

My siblings and I all trod off to 12 years of Catholic school taught by the IHM nuns (Sisters Servants of the Immaculate Heart of Mary). Only my eldest brother, Leo, tried to fight mother on this. He wanted to go to public school with his friends. He also thought it had a better football team. He won the battle for one year, attending West Pittston High School as a freshman. But no one won a war with my mother. She insisted that Leo would go to St. John's in Pittston for the remainder of high school.

Mother was influenced by her brother the priest, whom we called Father Leo. He insisted that good Catholic parents send their children to Catholic schools. This is not the only instance when our priest uncle gave direction for what was right and wrong with the way his sisters and brothers were raising their children.

At the age of seven, I wanted to join the local Brownie troop. Although Mother thought it would be a good experience for me, her support faltered when she learned that the meetings were held in the Baptist Church basement. The Baptist Church was less than a block away from our house. The church did not sponsor the troop but generously gave them the space to meet. Mother talked this over with the pastor, Father O'Brien, as well as her brother the priest, always believing that their word was the right one. In this case it reinforced the animosity that existed between the Catholics and Protestants in our little town of West Pittston. I went to one troop meeting but, before the next week, Mother firmly lectured me, "You, young lady, are not going to the Brownies in that Baptist Church."

"Why, Mother? All my friends are going. I want to be a Brownie."

"Father Leo and Father O'Brien said you cannot go in that Protestant church. It is forbidden by the Pope."

I tried to argue my way because one of my good friends, who was also Irish Catholic and lived right behind our house, had no problem with the venue. "Ann Devers is going. Why can't I?"

It just didn't make sense to this seven-year-old. We lived in a small town of 5,000 people with a church on almost every corner. Since I had now been inside the forbidden Baptist Church, curiosity about the remaining Protestant churches in our town grew in me. About two years later, it got the best of me. Why are Catholics forbidden to enter a Protestant church? At that time, our Immaculate Conception parish had a rather small church of painted white wood. But the inside was filled with statues, and a beautiful mural of the Blessed Virgin stood high above the stone altar. What were the Protestant churches like?

I didn't understand why we were forbidden to enter the big Protestant churches in our town and, like all kids faced with the forbidden, my nosiness got the best of me. What were they like? Each of these churches was within two to three blocks of our home and, since my sister Maureen and I had nothing else to do that summer afternoon when we, ages seven and nine, I dragged her along with me.

A church that always made us wonder what it was like inside was the Presbyterian church, only a block away from our house in the opposite direction of the Baptist church. The outside structure of the Presbyterian church extended over a half-block and, in the past, we would walk by and rub its red stone, which would leave a red powder on our fingers. For two young girls, its large, magnificent black iron door was there to be opened, and so, we snuck up the five stone steps to the entry. Together, we pushed.

Inside, we shivered with the cold dampness, even though it was summertime. Maureen, with her hand to her bright red curly hair, and quite excited, exclaimed, "This is almost like our church. Look at all the pews and the kneelers, and Jesus in that window and the altar. It's just like ours."

As we cautiously approached the altar, we saw beautiful candelabras set with unlit candles. The damp atmosphere gave off an odor of dankness. We giggled at the smell, but were sharply stunned by a voice coming from behind the altar, "What can I do for you young ladies?" We scampered to the front and scooted down those stairs and out the door to hide around the corner out of sight. We laughed and giggled that we made it safely without getting into trouble. We promised each other that this was our secret. We knew if we opened our mouths, we would be in big trouble at home.

Mother not only loved her mother, Nana, but she behaved as though Nana could do no wrong. If Nana did it, Mother would do it. Nana taught her children to be "Irish proud." We were not allowed to date anyone who was not Irish and certainly not to marry a non-Irish or a non-Catholic. We had to follow all the rules of the Irish Catholic priests who required adherence in the strictest terms to the Church catechism. Sometimes it was difficult to discern which were Irish rules and which were the Catholic Church rules.

Mother, much more than Dad, imposed strict and narrow-minded rules on our family. But she was always there to protect or defend us if anyone mistreated us. In elementary school, we all had one teacher for two grades. So even though we were not in the same grade, we could end up in the same classroom with a brother or sister.

Mary Clare and JoeJoe shared their fifth- and sixth-grade classrooms, presided over by mean old Sr. Damien. JoeJoe came home and told my mother that Sr. Damien had hit Mary Clare's head against the blackboard because she didn't know an answer. In no time, Agnes Granahan Jordan changed her dress; put on her heels; donned her coat, hat, and gloves; and, with a purse in hand, walked the half-mile to the convent. Knocking on the convent door, she was ready for battle. She let the principal know that Mary Clare came home with a headache, and who knows the damage that was done to her brain? I can only imagine my mother's words.

Even if you are not Catholic, you have probably heard the stories of how mean nuns can be. Sr. Damien was old, and that wasn't the first time her nerves got the best of her; she would often hit kids for misbehaving. Hitting a young girl of 12's head against the blackboard was the final straw for my mother. I do know that, after visiting the convent, she marched over to the priest's rectory and reported the incident to the pastor of the parish. He eventually had Sr. Damien transferred.

My mother always had our backs. She may sometimes have treated us like Attila the Hun but, when it came to right and wrong, she would always take up for justice and truth.

Because Maureen and I were inseparable playmates when we were growing up, we would often get into trouble and, when we did, as the elder, I carried the blame. When Nana was alive, Dad would drive the whole family over to Nana's home for dinner. Since there wasn't much for a two- and four-year-old to do, we would play outside. Dressed in our Easter Sunday best, we wandered behind the house to the anthracite coal dumps. What fun it was to run up and down the black culm mounds, falling and laughing as we climbed again.

In the distance, we heard calls that it was time to go home. We were a mess, blackened with coal dust from head to toe. Our Mary Jane shoes were no longer shiny patent leather; our beautiful Easter finery was full of soot. Mother was aghast.

"What am I going to do with you two? I'm going to throw you in the clothes washer and ring you through the wringer to get you clean. You have ruined your new dresses."

Frightened to death, I couldn't figure out how I could fit through those wringer rolls on the washer. Maureen and I both started to cry. When we went home, I remember spending time in the laundry room studying that old washer. It took a moment for me to learn that Mother could not be serious, and it was a great relief.

Maureen and I loved to play hopscotch until I barely started school. One day, Mother discovered us outside playing our favorite game at the time. We had chalked up the sidewalk, jumping and skipping from square to square, and having great fun. Oh, did we get it! Mother started hollering at us, scolding us for the mess we created on the sidewalk outside the tenants' door.

"Get a pail of water, a scrub brush, and a bar of soap, and scrub those walks until every inch of that chalk is gone. You will not chalk up our sidewalks."

If you have ever had to scrub chalk off a sidewalk or driveway, then you know how your fingers and knees get all scraped up, bleed, and burn. But we never complained, or our punishment would have been worse. That was the last time we played hopscotch. I believe that my mother was angry at something else that day and took it out on Maureen and me. Playing was what little kids like to do and there really wasn't any harm done.

THE ANGER GROWS

Often frustrated as a teenager, I struggled. Bold, bossy, sometimes belligerent, and always wanting to be heard, I often felt the same anger that churned in me in my mother.

During the summer that my sister Anne Marie was getting married, Mary Clare had just completed her first year of college, Maureen was entering junior high, and I had just completed my freshmen year of high school. The summer was our time for fun, but we were taking much guff from my mother, whose nerves were constantly on edge because of the wedding. The house needed to be spotless for the wedding reception. Our basement—actually a bare stone cellar floor and white-washed stone walls with a coal bin, a potato bin for root vegetables, and a brand-new oil-fueled furnace—was to hold a rectangular dance floor and a Victrola record player providing the music.

My father borrowed chairs from Charlie Donnelly, the undertaker, and scattered them throughout the house. My brothers packed ice chests on the enclosed back porch. Aunts and cousins prepared the food. Dad and all the uncles purchased the liquor for the Irish celebration. Everything had to be painstakingly arranged. Nellie, our dressmaker, designed and stitched our attendant dresses and frequently demanded our presence for fittings. Each one of us had a heavy schedule to keep.

We all carried the bride's burden. Anne Marie worked in Washington D.C. and did not come home until the week before her wedding. I found a cigar in Anne Marie's former bedroom, and I dared my sisters, Mary Clare and young Maureen, to smoke it. Assured that our mother was out of sight and hearing, we lit the cigar and attempted to pass it around among the three of us. Having inherited my mother's olfactory nerve, I now know why she suddenly appeared when the cigar was in my mouth and the smoke was choking me.

My sisters laughed hysterically until their faces turned ashen as Mother grabbed the cigar out of my mouth with one hand, and slapped me with her other across my face. I can't remember whether she said or did anything to Mary Clare or Maureen. I did not wait around to find out. Furious, I ran down the stairs and out the front door, towards the river and over the bridge, dropping tears along the way, ending up in St. John's Church where I consoled myself with God. Mother never apologized, and it took me many years to forgive that slap. Undoubtedly, it reinforced the angry me.

At the beginning of my sophomore year in high school, shortly after the cigar incident and on the advice of her brother the priest, Mother declared that I had to quit the high school majorette squad.

"It is not becoming for the niece of a priest to be showing her legs with those short skirts," she explained, evidently quoting her brother. (Short, really? They were just at the knee. They were approved by our principal, Father Gerrity.) I didn't understand. Having spent my whole freshman year preparing for the try-out, and winning a position on the squad as a sophomore put me over the moon.

My ire seethed, and I did not let this go. I took every opportunity that my blind young mind could think of to convince my mother how wrong this was. I turned to my father, but he remained silent because arguing with my mother about her brother the priest was a lost cause. I complained to my Auntie Mary, my mother's only living sister and her closest friend, begging her to convince my mother to change her mind.

Auntie was a schoolteacher who understood how important this was to me and agreed to do her part. "I'll talk to her, dear, but I don't know if she'll change her mind." Mother did not change her mind. She and Auntie had two different views of their brother's power. Auntie followed all the church rules if they were rules. The priest's word was good enough for Mother. When Auntie's pleas didn't work, I begged my friends' mothers to intercede, but that got me nowhere.

Finally, my dad said, "Enough. It's over." I pouted and continued to fuel the house with burning tension.

Aunt Mary, My Salvation

Aunt Mary decided that my mother and I both needed a break. She and her husband, Joe Murphy, asked me to stay with them for a week, hoping that would calm me down. I loved my aunt, and I knew she loved me. One night, this dear Auntie put me in her car, and we drove out into a rural area where the cornfields were high and no one was in sight. She walked me among the cornrows and said, "Honey, I want you to stand here and scream it out. Scream at your mother and Father Leo and anyone else you want to scream at, and do it loud. I want you to get it out of your system."

At first I couldn't do it. It seemed stupid. I opened my mouth, and nothing would come out. I tried again with a whisper, "I hate my mother." Auntie encouraged, "That's it, but louder." It did not come easy. Each time that followed got stronger until I screamed at the top of my lungs, "It's not fair. You knew for a whole year that I wanted to be a majorette. You knew how important this was to me, Mother. I hate you. I hate Father Leo. (That was sacrilegious.) He's not our boss!" I broke down into tears, sobbing all the way back to the house. Auntie told me as we drove back to the house that, when she was a young girl, she used to walk over to the cornfields and scream when she was angry, and it helped her.

My Auntie Mary provided some welcome balance to my mother's strictness with us. She was frequently over at our house, as we were at hers, and was a major influence in my life. She was strong in her Irish faith, but I recognized that she possessed an empathy that my mother did not have. At the age of 44, married four years to Joe Murphy, she gave birth to twins. One twin, Joseph, died at birth, and the second, Francis, was born with cerebral palsy. Raising Frankie Murphy was an enormous challenge. He could not raise his head until he was three, and only then because of Auntie's loving devotion that helped him to develop. Frankie was like a brother to us, and we were all his caretaker assistants.

Despite his severe handicaps of speech and hearing, Frankie was quite bright. Although sometimes frustration set in, he was a happy, joyous child whose smiles always tickled our hearts. He would appreciate a joke from an early age and would tease us in return. We were learning from Frankie how to be grateful for our gifts. Neither Frankie nor we were ever allowed a pity party.

Often Auntie would leave Frankie at our house with so many to care for him and take one or two of us to Wilkes-Barre shopping, followed by a lunch. Mary gave each of us girls incredibly special attention on these jaunts, especially if it was on our birthdays or other special occasions. Auntie took me by myself one Saturday to celebrate that I got my first menstrual period. She wanted to hear all about it because it happened during school. As I sat at the table with my head down feeling quite ashamed of something I did not understand and was not prepared for, Auntie took my hands to get my attention. With loving eyes, she told me how wonderful it was that I had become a woman. She was there for me when I needed her, a gift of respect and trust I have always treasured.

Auntie Mary demonstrated her courage and strength with raising her Frankie. But it was her affection, her love, her caring concern that smoothed out those angry sides of me. She stepped in when she knew my mother had probably gone too far and I needed some understanding. She never contradicted my mother, but she gave me the support I needed to become who I was.

Our cousins on my mother's side all tell the same stories of the strict discipline with which they were raised. Whether it was the Granahans in Philadelphia or those Granahans only three blocks from our house in West Pittston, we all learned that an Irish Catholic upbringing was tough, but also filled with love.

CHAPTER THREE

Mother's Other Voice

MOTHER WAS NOT A RUBE IN A SHAWL; she was far more compli-
cated. Giving birth to eight, one stillborn, and suffering three
miscarriages seemed to imprison who she was. I do not believe that
she loved motherhood very much or found joy in it. It was her calling,
"God's will," her obligation. Did she enjoy being a wife? Sometimes,
perhaps. I remember once that she giggled when my father "goosed"
her. I had just stuck my head through the kitchen door and there was
my father's hand on my mother's booty, both unaware of my presence.
She was enjoying it, laughing, while Daddy was teasing her. I found
her enjoyment puzzling since I had always seen her as serious. And
she never talked about sex with us unless it was to forewarn us about
getting pregnant.

Although Mother was serious about disciplining us, both she and Dad
were equal in their devotion to our education. Dad assured that we all sat
down at the kitchen or dining room tables every night to do our homework. He would hustle us after dinner to clean up, pick up the dishes,
assign the oldest girl to wash, and two girls to dry and put everything
away. Then it was homework time. He insisted that mother walk into the
living room, sit in her red lounge chair, close her eyes, and nap. "Agnes,"
he would say. "You've done enough today. I'll handle the homework."

Dad would hang out at the table with us when we needed help with
our assignments. He was good at math and especially liked dealing
with our math problems. Mother would eventually wake up from that
lounge chair and supervise our preparation for the next day of school.
She would try to work with us, one by one, for the next day's spelling
or reading tests.

With all the hardness of her Catholic upbringing, Mother did demonstrate, although not often, her loving physical side. I recall a frigid day in northeastern Pennsylvania as I arrived home for lunch with freezing hands. Standing between the hot radiator and the warm stove as she stirred the soup, Mother encouraged me to put my hands under her arms. "This will warm them very quickly." And it warmed those hands and my heart.

Because I had so many brothers and sisters older than me, I picked up reading at an early age. Often before I went to bed, Mother would sit on her bed and have me read to her. She took great pride in my ability to read so early, and I loved that special time with her.

Agnes Jordan also believed in supporting the church, the school, and the community. As a member and president of the Altar and Rosary Society for several years, she formed many women friendships. For the 14 years one of us was in high school, she was an active member of the Mothers Club. Each election cycle would find Mother and Dad volunteering at the polls for the Democratic Party. Until she was 93 years old, and her eyesight diminished, she held the position of judge of election in our precinct.

When Mother was 90 and I was 53, I had a special moment with her at a dinner in historic Williamsburg, Virginia. She had never been there and was thrilled that we could make this trip together. After a day of pushing her wheelchair in and out of the colonial shops and through the gravel, I welcomed our evening of relaxation in the dining room of the Williamsburg Inn. Nursing my Johnny Walker Black on the rocks and she, her cherished "nothing but Christian Brothers" brandy, I asked Mother why she waited so long to be married. She dated my father for seven years and was 28 when they wed, rather old for that period when women were married before they were 20. She answered, "I guess I hoped someone better would come along." Her response was intriguing. I asked, "Did you ever love Dad?"

"I guess I did," was her response.

She then asked me, "What do you think about abortion?" Gobsmacked, I had to think quickly. I believed in a woman's right to choose. Is that what she wanted to hear? So, I lobbed back to her, "What do you think about it?"

"Well, if I believed in abortion, you wouldn't have been born." I laughed, but a stab hit my brain — she didn't want so many kids. She continued, "These priests think they know everything, but they know nothing about what it is like for a woman." I found an opening and explained that I never had to decide on abortion, but I did believe in every woman's right to choose. My father had been dead a year when we had this conversation.

I recalled another time when Mother asked me, "Do you believe there's a heaven?" Oh, my God, was this woman (who spent nine decades holding firm to Catholic beliefs handed down from her mother) now questioning the basics? She had just lost my father, her sister Mary, and her brother, Father Leo, within six weeks. I had to be truthful. She was struggling.

"I believe that there is another life. That the souls, the spirits of Daddy, Mary, and Father Leo are out there somewhere. I'm not sure about 'heaven and hell.' But I believe in God."

She then asked me, "Why?" I took some time to ponder and respond.

"Mom, it's a matter of believing, not knowing. But I've had certain things happen to me that have strengthened my belief. You have believed all of your life. I've learned a lot about religion in the convent. I've also had some experiences that make me believe there's life after this one on earth. I believe that there is another world. Perhaps that's what we call heaven."

I then told her some stories which you will hear later. I'm not sure I gave her any strength against her doubts, but she did show some interest in my stories.

When we were young, we all knelt around with Dad and said our prayers. As we grew older, the prayers of children grew into the rosary, as Father Peyton came on the scene with his campaign, "The Family That Prays Together, Stays Together." My dad believed in this mantra. If any of our friends popped in before we were finished, all were welcome and were expected to kneel in the living room with us and join in the prayers. We were not excused until the rosary was finished. Although Dad was the leader in prayer, Mother was also committed to the rosary as she was to everything Catholic.

Dad had been a member of the Knights of Columbus and even became a Fourth Degree Knight and the Grand Knight of the Pittston club. The Knights of Columbus was a connection he made in the community to build his construction business. Most of the members of the Knights of Columbus were of Irish descent. The Knights, even with God on their side, were not as powerful as the Italian Mafia. But the Knights club was a drinking place, and Dad enjoyed his liquor. Many tense arguments ensued between Dad and Mother about his drinking.

One of the saddest days I remember was when I was about ten. Mother arranged with Dad's brother, Uncle Jimmy (an ophthalmologist), her brother Jack Granahan, and Father Leo to insist that my father take the "pledge" to stop drinking. Johnny, Maureen, and I (only six, eight, and ten, and the youngest in the family) were sent over to my Auntie Mary's to clear our house for this planned intervention. I had overheard many conversations between my parents, with Mother insisting, "Joe, you can't go on drinking like this. I want you to go and see Father O'Brien and take the pledge." The pledge was a promise to the Sacred Heart that originated in Ireland at the turn of the 20th century. A society called "The Pioneers" was sanctioned by the Irish Catholic Church to enlist Irish men to stop drinking alcohol for the rest of their lives. This pledge was a vow to God, and American Irish Catholics were often induced to take this pledge to control their drinking.

Although perhaps too young to understand the fullness of what they were demanding of my dad, I understood how broken and embarrassed he was. I knew that Daddy was the target of the gossip in that block of relatives. I had heard the neighbor-cousins questioning Auntie Mary.

Johnny, Maureen, and I were peeking through the maple banisters on the staircase. We had been on the second floor playing, and we snuck down when we heard the cars outside. As the leader, I knew we were not supposed to be there, but I needed to hear what they had to say. My heart ached for Dad as the cloud of depression, despair, and humiliation surrounded his entire being with head bent, eyes lowered, energy drained. Frightened, I could not voice my questions, my distress, my empathy. Was Daddy going to be okay?

Despite the intervention, Dad drank most of his life. Some of my father's seven siblings also drank heavily. The Irish have a rap for loving the "bit of."

I realize that my mother and I could never see eye to eye on this intervention. I sensed that Mother, as a wife, viewed this pledge as her last hope. As she would say, she was "at her wit's end." She pleaded, cajoled, cried, and blamed Dad for the results of his drinking. She hated it. The only time my father appeared to be angry at her was when she continued her nagging at him. Then I wondered, what role did she play in his need for drinking? Was it the nagging, not just about drinking, but it seemed it was the books he read, his friends, and even his siblings?

I still hold close my belief that the "pledge" does not work. The humiliation to the drinker may be beyond repair. Mother and Dad fulfilled their marriage vows to each other for 60 years. So, could Mother have found another more supportive voice that might have worked?

CHAPTER FOUR

Books, Books, Books

I OFTEN WONDERED IF EVERYONE LOVED BOOKS as much as I did. I relished being away from reality and entering into the lives of other young girls: *Anne of Green Gables, Rebecca of Sunnybrook Farm, Alice's Adventures in Wonderland, Heidi, Jane Eyre, Charlotte's Web, Black Beauty* and, of course, the writer Jo and her sisters in *Little Women*. Curious about other lands and other cultures, I explored with Nancy Drew, Treasure Island, The Little Prince, Huckleberry Finn, and *The Adventures of Tom Sawyer.*

Our local library was my place of respite. A small, red brick building situated on a quiet street only two blocks from the Susquehanna River, the library was warm and welcoming with tall, dark wood bookcases and hardwood floors. I loved walking through the tree-lined streets skipping among the cracks on the concrete sidewalks. Smelling the honeysuckle as I neared the building sent thrills up my spine.

Checking out a book at the library for the first time at the age of seven and asking for a library card was not a happy experience for me. The librarian was quite helpful as I canvassed the Nancy Drew section, helping me pick out three volumes which she said I could have for two weeks. When I was ready to check out, and after I had given the librarian my name and address for my library card, she asked me, "Is Anne Marie Jordan your sister?" I looked up with bright eyes and a toothless grin as I answered with an enthusiastic, "Oh, yes. Do you know my sister? She has pretty red hair."

She smiled but her voice was stern, "She has a book that she has not returned for over a year, so I cannot let you take these books until the book is returned and the fine paid." I was devastated. I stared at those books as she placed them on the table behind her. My heart sank. I had chosen them so carefully and was excited to read the stories.

I looked up at her with tears streaming down my little face trying to convince her. I felt that this was unfair. It wasn't my fault, so why was I being punished?

"My sister did that, not me. I don't think that's fair."

Miss Douglas reached over and took my hand in her two hands and apologized. "I'm so sorry. It doesn't seem fair to you. I understand, dear. If you tell your mother, I'm sure she'll take care of this, and you will have your card and be able to read these books very soon."

I tried once more. "Please let me take these books out. I promise I will return them. I'll tell my mother, and we will get the book back to you." It seems I could not stop begging her for those books.

"I'm sorry, honey, but that's the way it's done. If the family owes money, then no one in that family gets to take out a book. I'm sorry. But if you tell your parents, I'm sure they'll handle it, and you'll be able to get your card."

She continued identifying the name of the book, which I do not remember, and the fine of a penny a day for 380 days. I could not believe it. In 1945, the minimum wage was 40 cents per hour. At this time my father's business was doing well. We had the money, but my mother was going to be very mad. I cried and cried all the way home. Between the tears, I tried to figure out what I could do to get my sister to find the book and bring it back. At 15, Anne Marie did some babysitting, but did she have this much money? We children were always responsible for our debts.

As I expected, no one was happy. Anne Marie just shrugged her shoulders, so Mother just started yelling at her.

"Find that book now. Until I see it in my hands, you are not going out tonight." I gave Anne Marie the note with the name of the book and how much she owed.

Anne Marie found the book, but it seemed to take her forever. She then stared Mother down with. "I don't have any money for this book."

Mother finally said, "I will give Aggie that money tomorrow when she returns the book, and you will pay me back every penny."

The next morning, I skipped my way back with book and money in hand. Miss Douglas handed me my card and my books. My reading life had begun

My parents bought us a set of World Book Encyclopedias. Even though it was a burdensome expense, they were willing to take it on because World Book allowed them to pay it with monthly payments. Paying things off over time was a new experience for my parents. But they valued education for us, and they understood that these books would be a ready reference for our school assignments.

I was so excited and waited each day for the delivery. I would check the front porch when I arrived home from school. "No, Aggie, it didn't come today," my mother would say in exasperation. It seemed to me that it took forever for those books to arrive. And when they came, I was allowed to unbox those 25 dark blue treasures with silver engraving and display them on the shelf in the living room. As the days passed, I was thrilled that I could pick any book right there in my house at any time. I secretly made a promise to myself to read every page of every volume. I'm not sure that I finished every page of every volume, but when I got to the last book of WXYZ, I closed that book with a thrill of accomplishment. Yes, I did it.

Books also became my refuge in high school after my parents refused to let me be a majorette. I read incessantly, much to the dismay of my brothers and sisters who did not understand how I could be absorbed into a world that kept me from the reality around us. For most of my years, at least five of us were always fighting for our own space. Because each of us had our friends, and with neighborhood kids and relatives dropping in and out, I had to search for my own quiet space for reading.

Often Mary Clare and JoeJoe would find me in a corner in Mom and Dad's bedroom, behind the piano in the music room, or in the kitchen closet that enclosed the staircase to the apartment we rented out on the third floor. They would make every effort to distract me, joking, singing, making faces, and even taunting me. One day, with a glass of milk in one hand and a book in the other, I am told that my brother, JoeJoe, took the milk from my hand as I kept on reading undisturbed. Yes, in these nooks and corners, I found my reading life. I was able to concentrate on reading and ignore their presence and focus without distraction.

China and Japan caught my curiosity when I was a 12-year-old.. Searching out as much as I could find on these countries, I explored through brochures, maps, and the encyclopedia to imagine what life was like in these foreign lands. I read about the Maryknoll sisters and priests who were dedicated to helping people there. I thought how exotic their lives were helping those Chinese children. I could see those Chinese faces, just like the ones on our Lenten penny savings card. We filled those cards every Lent to save the hungry Chinese kids. Exotic, yes, I wanted to learn more. I sent away for literature inquiring about what their lives were like. I wanted to be a Maryknoll nun and go to China.

Father Leo was cautious in his response when I shared my interest in the Maryknoll sisters. Taking his finger and pressing it into my shoulder, he said, "Pray on that. It's a hard life to be a missionary. I don't think you would like it." I was disappointed. I wanted him to share in my excitement. I hated that finger. It meant, "Don't do it."

"Why would it be hard," I asked? "I think living in a foreign land would be fun."

"No, Aggie, it wouldn't be fun. It would be God's work, but you would be away from everyone and everything familiar here. You might not see your family for a very long time. And it's dangerous. You don't know those people."

As I took up the challenge of what I would do with my life after entering my senior year in high school, going to China was no longer an interest. My interests became more real. What did I truly want in life?

Books had taught me to be the best I could be. I wanted others to be proud of me, especially my mother and father. What could one do to please them, especially my mother? What would be her greatest satisfaction for a child of hers? What was the epitome of success in this Irish Catholic family? Not only for my parents, but also for the old Irish clan? Of course, it was always the Church.

CHAPTER FIVE

Time's Up. Decide!

Hanging around after school, I prepared with the debate team. I helped with the yearbook because most of my friends were involved in its production and my boyfriend, Ed, was the editor. Ed was an excellent student and Irish. No guff from my family about him as my boyfriend. As my 17-year-old hormones seethed through my body, I loved being with him. But being disciplined Irish Catholic kids, we knew that kissing was as far as we would go.

I joined my friends in whatever trouble we could get into without our parents finding out. For a while, we believed that if we put aspirin in our Cokes, we would get a high. That's about as much as we knew about drugs. Cigarettes were another story.

In the basement restrooms of Pittston City Hall, which was a block from our high school entrance, my girlfriends and I would go to smoke after we ate lunch. We were juniors and thought we were quite sophisticated. This cigarette habit advanced to a cigarette and Coke after school and sometimes to riding around in a van with our boyfriends. Although the nuns never chastised me, my mother's voice never let up when she smelled the smoke on my breath or my clothes.

"It wasn't me, Mom. It was the guys in the van that were smoking." I stood face to face and denied the fact.

"Don't lie to me, young lady. I could smell it when you came in through that front door." I knew she wasn't buying my story. I would just have to learn to hide it better.

Sometime in the last semester of my senior year, my daily prayers focused on what I wanted to do with my life. My thoughts were constantly about the future. I just couldn't figure out what I wanted to do. I knew I wanted to go to college, but I had no goal. What would I study? Most of my dear friends were going to one of the five local colleges. To go away to college was out of the question for all of us. It was just too expensive.

I would constantly send up a cry, "Jesus, please help me to know what you want me to do with my life. Holy Spirit, guide me." My prayers became more intense as the school year came to a close. I needed direction for my life. I had attended daily Mass for most of my young years. I believed in the power of Divine Providence. God loved me and would provide for me. God the Father would take care of me. I believed strongly that he would show me the way. I believed in Jesus Christ and that he lived on this earth as our model to find our way. I believed in heaven and hell because that was what I was taught for 12 years.

I was not afraid of heaven or hell. I don't believe I ever thought about God as the punisher. I saw God as more like my own gentle and loving father. But these beliefs didn't seem to be helping me decide. My mother just assumed that I would go to a local college. I applied hoping I would receive a few scholarships, and if I got a job, I could make it work. I wasn't thrilled about living at home, but that was the viable option.

At times, especially during the quiet of morning Mass, as I knelt in my pew staring at the altar lit with those burning candles, I would think about joining the convent. As the year went on, the nagging thought became more powerful. Sometimes I would just shake my head and dismiss it. At other times, I would say, "Really, Jesus, why do you want me?"

I did not make any inquiries of the nuns at this point about what life might be like for them. This struggle was between God and me. What did he want me to do? All I knew of my teachers was that they were with us during the day and then went home to a building that we called a convent. I had only been inside a convent when I took piano lessons from the nuns. The little music room that was barely big enough for a black upright piano was at the convent's side entrance. I would take off my coat, open my music book, and immediately sit down at the piano and begin my finger exercises. At one end of the room was a door that was always closed except to open and close when Sr. Mercia, my piano teacher, joined me.

Once I was early for a music lesson, and Sister Mercia greeted me and ushered me into the chapel.

"Come, follow me into the chapel. You can sit here and pray while I finish with this lesson." As I sat in the chapel, I could hear the piano sound of a youngster not very far along in her lesson. Every other note seemed off key. Soon that off-key music was dulled. I liked being in the chapel. It was small with an altar dressed in a white linen cloth with candelabras on each end. Facing the altar were six prie-dieu. I absorbed the quiet, the silence of Jesus' presence, as I knelt there before the altar. Then my mind would wander. Where did the nuns eat? Where did they sleep? I never got the answers to those questions as a grade school pianist.

Even at 17, I knew nothing about their lives, about the vows of poverty, chastity, and obedience. I knew they took these vows and that they would never marry. They didn't look very poor to me. They seemed to have everything they needed. Everybody I knew was always giving them things. I knew my dad often brought them a bottle of whiskey.

Was it even possible for me to understand fully at 17 the sacrifices a nun's life would demand? I don't remember any deep thoughts about living with women for the rest of my life. Did I feel that joining the convent was the only way to be revered by my mother? I don't know these answers. But today these questions make me wonder whether I considered very deeply what it meant to be a nun at this time in my young life. If God was calling me, that would be all that mattered.

College acceptances came with a few scholarships, and I followed them up with visits to the campuses, but nothing seemed to turn me on. I didn't know what I wanted for my future. Choices were quite limited for young women in 1955: a nurse, a teacher, a secretary, or a wife. None of these attracted me, not even teaching, which was the most frequent occupation for women in my family. It would have been the most likely choice.

A few of our high school mates would talk about getting married, but that was far from what any one of my friends had in mind. I did not want to be married at such a young age, tied to a man like chattel, looked down upon because I am female. I did not want to be my mother, never fulfilling her dreams, "settling" because no one better came along. What effect did my mother's anger and unhappiness, my parents' arguments, and the knowledge that marriages weren't necessarily happy have on me? I remember saying to my mother when I finally shared with her my decision to join the convent, "I don't think I ever want to get married." Her failure to respond to this bold admission made me think that she understood, even perhaps if I didn't.

Many of my women friends tell me that they always knew they wanted children. I can't remember ever having that deep urge. Perhaps in this way, my mother and I were alike. She had them, but did she want them? At some point, I thought I wanted a career in medicine. Science was not my strongest achievement in school, yet I looked for something that would help me do something unusual for a woman.

GOD'S CALL

I can't be sure of how the call came. Perhaps it was through my daily attendance at Mass. I would not need an alarm. I would wake up before dawn so that I could go to the 7 a.m. Mass at St. John's. I would head out into the cold, grey skies in winter and walk the mile over the bridge across the Susquehanna River. Snow or rain, I did not miss Mass unless I was sick. I knelt in St. John's Church before the Mass began, praying for help. The candles were lit on the altar; my friends had not yet arrived to join me, and I had all the morning quiet necessary to get God's attention.

Why was God silent? Or was I not listening to what God wanted? I was fighting what I knew God wanted for me in my heart — to be a nun. Suddenly I knew that to give myself to Jesus would be enormous. I knew that nuns were considered to be the brides of Christ. Yes, God the Father was my caretaker, God the Son, Jesus, was the one who came to this earth to be like us and who died for me. And God the Holy Spirit, I kind of pictured him as my "Spirit," that which gave me wisdom and intelligence. I would pray always to the Holy Spirit because I thought of him as Intelligence, and he rested inside me like my own spirit. We had a song that we often sang in church that I would use as my prayer when I needed the Holy Spirit's guidance:

> *Come Holy Spirit, Creator Blest*
> *And in our hearts take up thy rest*
> *Come with thy grace and heavenly aid*
> *To fill the hearts which thou hast made.*

However, it was Jesus, and the Father, who took care of me. Oh, how exasperated my mind was when it tried to examine this Trinitarian concept of God. The nuns and priests always told us it was a mystery. No doubt about that. Yet I continued to pray to each of the Trinity for guidance as though I understood that mystery.

Days and weeks passed, and I still had doubts. Was this pressure to join the convent an idealistic drive to choose a high calling encouraged by my family, school, and church? I understood that choosing the convent would please a lot of people. Yet I questioned whether giving my life to God was what I wanted to do. That nagging thought of joining the convent would not leave me alone. I continued to pray that I would know God's will for me.

Hesitant, even nervous, about approaching any of the nuns, I didn't even confide in any of my girlfriends about what I was thinking. There was no high school counselor, and I felt no inclination to talk to a confessor. I had no one I felt I could trust. Finally, I drummed up the courage to approach my science teacher. Sister Clarice was young, and I liked her joyful personality. She had a broad smile and very white teeth with big brown eyes that danced through those horse blinders. She seemed happy, and I felt she would respect my confidence. From her I learned about life in the convent. Jesus' words, "Leave your father and mother and everything you have and come follow me," were what motivated her. Through my conversations with Sr. Clarice, I clearly heard God's call. She spoke to my heart. I understood the message as my call. It didn't matter if this call meant I had to give up everything. Jesus was doing the calling.

I did not want my family or any of my friends to know, especially my boyfriend, until after graduation. I wanted to have a good time. I didn't want anyone to put me in the convent before I got there, to treat me differently. During the summer, Ed went to Naval Reserve training, and we wrote back and forth several times. My relationship with him was the most difficult part of my decision. I cared for him, but I knew I was not ready to love anyone intimately at 17.

Having to give up Ed was the ambivalence that kept me from taking any action earlier. When I told him in the summer after he returned from his Naval Reserve duty, he made it easy for me. I entered the convent without ever having another conversation with him.

Telling my closest friends was also difficult. I loved being with them; and giving up their friendship, perhaps forever, made me rethink my decision. I hesitated to tell them, not only because it would be the last time I would talk to them, but also because I felt guilty about not having mentioned anything to them before. My dearest and most intelligent friend, Aggie McDermott, questioned why I wanted to do this. "Why do you want to be a nun? I can't imagine you a nun." I just could not give her a good answer except, "I don't know. God seems to be calling me." Another dear friend, Peggy McTigue, who loved life and partying just thought I was crazy, "Why would you give up boys? You like them. I could never give up boys."

I didn't tell them because I didn't trust myself. I don't know if I was sure until I told them. After the words stumbled out of my mouth, I was confident. Then again, perhaps I didn't trust anyone with what I considered my secret, even my parents. Up until I told my friends and family, it was my struggle with my conscience which was forcing me to answer the call. Once I admitted to what I wanted and was going to do, a very private decision became a very public one.

When I told my mother I wanted to join the convent, she hugged me, and the tears covered her face. "God calling my child. I can't believe it. Such a blessing. You have to go and tell your father." She was thrilled, but my father was less so.

"Are you sure that's what you want?"

"Dad, I've been thinking about it a long time. I've been going to Mass every day and praying for God to tell me what to do."

"If you're sure, you have my blessing." I knew he would not interfere if he thought it was God's will. He asked me to rethink it to be sure that was what I wanted to do. I shared that I had been struggling with this decision, praying over it for many months, and I was sure.

Auntie Mary was overjoyed, but her husband, Uncle Joe, took the air out of me when he said, "You know you have never liked anyone to tell you what to do. When you go there, you're going to have to do what they tell you. I don't think you're going to like that. I hope you understand that."

Uncle Joe struck a chord in me. For a moment I questioned, "Was this decision right for me? Why would he say this to me?" I didn't know what to say. Deep in my heart, I felt that he understood something about my joining the convent that I had not faced. If there was one moment, it was then that I committed to Jesus, God the Father, and the Holy Spirit that I was doing this. Yes, I would obey. Whatever it took, I was going to be a nun.

Telling my siblings did not seem to be a big deal. The older ones were already into their own lives. Leo and Anne Marie were married and living out of town. Mary Clare was graduating from college and getting ready to teach. JoeJoe had joined the Army.

Maureen and Johnny were closer to me, and they had a different take. Maureen remembers how much joy I had, and it seemed right for me. Three years later, she followed me into religious life, joining my community. She stayed for about 18 months, through the first year of the novitiate. She tells me that, through that whole time, she had doubts about her choice. "Why am I here?" was a question she often asked herself, until she finally came up with the answer: "I shouldn't be."

Johnny recently celebrated his 50th anniversary as a priest in the Diocese of Scranton, a life he has given particularly to the education of youth. But a question lingers with me: why did the youngest three in that family of seven feel they were called to religious life? How different was our upbringing from our four older siblings? Was it because we three grew up in the "poor phase" of my father's work life? And the phase when my mother was so unhappy, and my dad felt less than the man he knew he should be? What was it about that period of our lives that influenced our being led toward religious life? I wish I knew the answer to that puzzle.

PART TWO

The Convent

CHAPTER SIX

Preparing to Leave My Family

I READ THE LIST OF INSTRUCTIONS to prepare for entering the convent, and this long inventory gave me second thoughts. This didn't seem right. The list of clothes to bring was really scary. I had to buy two pairs of black oxfords with chunky heels. Of course, black cotton stockings were necessary to accompany them. Shopping for the underwear was an embarrassing experience. My sister, Mary Clare, came with me to shop for those full grandma panties, men's undershirts, and full cotton bras. Was I giving up being a girl?

Ashamed to think I would have to wear these not very girlie unmentionables, the shopping trip was no fun. We borrowed Dad's car and headed for Lazarus Department Store ten miles away in Wilkes-Barre. Mary Clare worked there all through her college years, both nights and weekends, so she knew exactly where we would find these items. Mary Clare had a great sense of humor and pulled me through each of the departments. I did not want to try on the bras and refused to try on the undershirts. Standing 5' 4" and weighing in at 115, I just took everything in the small sizes. Soon Mary Clare and I were both laughing. We joked that the convent would turn me into a man. Even my mother laughed when I brought these items home.

Another requirement was a dowry of $300. Luckily I had very generous aunts and uncles who threw me a "money shower" at their summer homes on the Susquehanna River in Harding, Pennsylvania. The haul was exactly $300. My mother and dad were truly pleased. It would have been a great burden for them to come up with that amount of money.

THE DAY ARRIVES

I can't remember what else I was required to bring with me, but it was all packed in the suitcase on September 8, 1955, when my mother, my sister Maureen, and my brother Johnny stood anxiously by me as my father rang the doorbell at the Marywood motherhouse.

We were greeted by the postulant mistress, Sister Gertrude Marie, who was warm and welcoming. Extending her arm from her short but rotund body, she greeted me with a kindly hug. Yet my nerves were electrifying every word I uttered, or step I took, as we entered this dark parlor with heavy antique furniture, hanging tapestries, and weighty dark red drapes decorating the floor-to-ceiling windows.

I calmed down when I saw a familiar face. A nun in a white veil came through the door, greeting me with a bright smile and "Aggie, I'm so glad you are joining us." I recognized her as the Kelly girl from Pittston who was two years ahead of me in high school, and I was happy to see someone I knew. She was assigned to take me into the inner sanctum where I would change from my summer clothes into the proper dress for recruits.

My family was allowed to enjoy themselves in the 17th century parlor with cookies and lemonade while Sister Gertrude Marie entertained them. When I appeared 30 minutes later all newly dressed, there was a stunned silence. There I stood in a black wool skirt with a waistband that held pleats falling well below the knees. A black cotton blouse with long sleeves and a mandarin collar was draped with a cape, topped off with a 1.5-inch white plastic collar. I was all in black with that speck of white. This was the dress of the newbie, an applicant called a postulant. My hair, covered with a black lace veil, gave some appearance of my being a nun. And yes, beneath all this was that underwear I had purchased. Whether it was the outfit or the anxiety that I was different now, I was uncomfortable standing there with my family.

My mother and Maureen clearly could not hold back the tears, I started to cry. Johnny broke the mood with "You don't look like a nun, but you sure look different," as my dad just stood there waiting for his hug. I had to hand them the suitcase I brought that held my pink knee-length cotton print sundress, feminine underwear, and sandals. Dad handed Sister Gertrude Marie the envelope with my dowry, and my family was ready to leave.

It was now dinnertime. If I had arrived earlier, they would have had more time to spend with me touring the grounds, but it was time for them to go. Mom's eyes were red, and she was wiping the tears away. Maureen hugged me, continued to tell me she was going to miss me. She and Johnny would now be alone with my parents. I would miss everyone, but I was ready. There were no more tears. I felt very much alone, but I had made a commitment and an adventure lay ahead.

CHAPTER SEVEN

The First Six Months

NO ONE HAD TOLD ME that the time one arrived dictated seniority, the position or status I would hold with my fellow postulants. Those who came from a distance, like Long Island, New York, had come the previous afternoon and would be assigned the earliest numbers that would identify them as holding the senior positions in the group. Five of them arrived together. There they sat at the long table surrounding the postulant mistress who was at the head. I envied their positions, their apparent comfort, and their cackle which seemed to take over the evening meal.

I only lived ten miles away. Frustrated, I thought, *if only I had known, I could have been here yesterday.* I would think Sr. Clarice, my high school sponsor, would have told me that important piece of information. Perhaps she did, and it didn't register with me. Or did I just ignore it because I wanted to wait until the last minute? As number 39 out of 40 to arrive, this fixed my position in the postulancy in the back of the room. At the dinner table that night, I sat near the end. One more young woman would arrive late that night.

At the end of the evening, each of us was given a number which we held for the rest of our days. The numbers in our group ranked from single digits to my four digits. We were instructed that in the morning someone would distribute to each of us one roll of cotton numbers and we would sew them on each item of our clothing.

In the beginning, all assignments were meted out by this ranking system. So, who were the first ones left with the kitchen duty team? Those of us at the end of the line. The postulants with lower numbers got the special assignments of leading the prayers and chapel duty, which entailed (among other things) preparing the altar for Mass and generally what I regarded as light assignments. I got some comfort when Sr. Gertrude Marie explained to us that our assignments would rotate while we were postulants so everyone would get a chance at the light ones and the heavy ones.

It wasn't fun to work in the kitchen. Two cooks directed the meal production. One was the chief chef, and the other was very determined that everyone should do her job silently. I don't remember the name of Sister #1, but I do remember #2, Sister Emerita. Sister #1 would often try to scare us into believing that the end of the world was coming soon. The nuclear bombs of World War II had grabbed her inner being, and she was convinced there would soon be a World War III. Her admonition was always, "Act as though this is your last day. Pray always while you peel the potatoes, wash the vegetables, peel the onions (worst job), and prepare the beef, chicken, fish, or seafood." I refused to believe in her fears. But, once in a while, I would hear another postulant say, "She could be right."

Although most of us thought Sister #1 was a little off her rocker, we did what she said. She often was a topic of our conversation as we stole moments to break the silence when we were sent to the basement for the huge cases of canned goods or bushels of potatoes. We would whisper, "Act as though this is our last day? She must be nuts. We just got here." Another would say, "She's talking about death or the end of the world."

When we were at recreation in the evening, we always had one jokester who would imitate her. "It's coming, it's coming. I just read the news. The end of the world is coming." We would all bend over with laughter, at the same time hoping that our postulant mistress would not ask us to repeat what we were so enjoying: "Share with us, ladies." Oops, then we knew we were in trouble.

One fun job was helping bake the bread. Sister Emerita was the baker, and I loved being her helper. Once a week, on Friday, we would prepare fresh homemade bread. That 115 pounds on me soon started to climb. No matter where you were on Friday, the smell of fresh bread wafted through the entire convent.

Sister Emerita was also aged in the eyes of 17-year-olds. She may have been in her mid to late 50s, very thin with deep-set eyes and an aquiline nose with plenty of wrinkles on the very few parts of the body that were exposed. She was tough, quick, and efficient as she delivered orders when we were assigned to her. She usually rose early to prepare breakfast and then would join the kitchen crew late in the afternoon.

Sister Emerita's primary duty was to be the seamstress to the motherhouse convent. When my turn to work in the sewing room came, I got to know her a little better. She appreciated that I knew how to sew, a skill my mother insisted that we all learn, even the boys. We girls often made some of our skirts and tops for school. The boys' skill was centered on threading a needle and sewing on their buttons or fixing a hem in their pants. Eventually, Sister would often ask for me to help her out when she was under pressure to meet some deadlines for finishing habits. She taught me how to cut and sew serge. She told me, much to my pleasant surprise, that she hoped I could be assigned to her when I became a novice. I enjoyed working with her because she would tell me stories of saints as we worked. It's difficult to describe how someone's holiness fills the atmosphere, but I felt peace in her presence. Plus, she was good for my ego.

Learning the language of this new culture was a challenge. Yes, everyone spoke English, but learning the vocabulary was like learning a new language. We 40 were known as a band, a term that distinguished us for the rest of our convent life. "What band were you in? 1955. Oh, that's the same one as Sister So-and-So," was the general chatter. The Great Silence was a new term but also a difficult concept. We were not to speak or non-verbally communicate with anyone after the bell rang for night prayers until after Mass the following morning. We kept our heads down and our eyes to ourselves. Well, we tried. It took us several days to be in tune with the Great Silence as some of us could not keep the smirks, smiles, and signals to ourselves.

Soon we learned that silence in the convent is a sacred prayer, and the Great Silence is a most holy time in preparation for attendance at the celebration of Mass and reception of the Holy Eucharist the next morning. The Great Silence was my time alone with God. I soon learned to treasure these moments that brought peace and prayerful thought to my life. It was for these moments that I joined the convent, to become closer to God.

Sister Gertrude Marie, who stood a rotund 5 feet tall, was a motherly postulant mistress who had the job of turning us into holy women. We came from all over the eastern United States, some from very wealthy families, some from poor backgrounds. A few were only children, but most of us were members of large families, all of us waiting to be melded into one uniform model of sanctity.

I enjoyed getting to know my fellow postulants, eating three healthy meals a day, even rising at five in the morning for prayers and Mass. *Tu autem domino miserere nobis* was the awakening voice of the novice assigned with the ringing bell and the knock on the 20-bed dormitories. The novice was saying, "But you, oh Lord, have mercy on us." Why, what had I done at 5 a.m. that I needed God's mercy? Our answer was to be *Deo Gratias et Maria*. That means, "Thanks be to God and Mary." Why am I thanking God and the Blessed Mother for getting up at five in the morning? It made no sense to me. Naturally, being inquisitive, I asked those questions of Sister Gertrude Marie.

"In time, dear, in time," was her answer.

I later learned that we were always asking God for his mercy. That wasn't so strange since it was common around our house to hear my mother or dad dejectedly saying, "Lord, have mercy," when we kids would make trouble. This, however, was different. Begging God's mercy was to make me humble. Even after 14 years of hearing these wake-up calls, I never did get the connection between begging His mercy and thanking Him for getting up. Nor probably did I learn much humility. This begging God for mercy so early in the morning was an enigma to all of us new ones. We usually joked about it for the first few weeks, but generally, it became such a habit that it was no longer important.

We had a half-hour to make it to "Morning Prayers" followed by Mass, so there was no dawdling. The first one up and out to the bathroom didn't have to wait her turn at the johns or the sinks. Showers happened the night before. This early morning rising became a joy for me: arriving early in the chapel with the candles glowing, the silence enveloping, and my very own moments to deepen my relationship with God.

It was in these moments of morning prayers and meditation that I learned to acknowledge the Holy Spirit and to develop a more intense relationship with Him. The Holy Spirit has no required gender to me. As a young girl, I never understood why if "I was made to the image and likeness of God," a long-held belief in the Catholic Church, why were all of God's images male? Nevertheless, I continued to believe in and communicate with the God I was taught to love. I made a private agreement with myself that God the Father and the Holy Spirit did not need gender. Since Jesus was born as a male, I accepted that. And this gender mystery of the Trinity was resolved in my young mind.

Our early morning instruction was both spiritual and practical. Our first day's lesson included the proper behavior in response to that rising call. Sister Gertrude Marie would train us to perform the simplest task of attendance at Mass or performing our household chores. I went to Mass every morning of my school life. I felt like I knew the rituals of Mass. Yet we all had to be in that same lecture on what to do. I had also done the housework rituals since I was ten. Granted, I didn't know how to make hospital corners on a bed, but I did know how to clean a house. I felt somewhat better prepared for the cleaning, dusting, vacuuming, and scrubbing floors and toilets than a number of my band members who never had to do anything in their homes. Some grew up with maids and nannies. Humility about what I knew how to do was not my strong point. But I would learn.

We received instruction about proper convent manners including how to eat an orange or where to put your unoccupied hand while eating, and what to do with your eyes when passing a senior sister in the hall. I have not forgotten how to eat an orange by cutting it in half with a knife and scooping the segments out with a fork, although I rarely, if ever, perform this ritual. My unoccupied hand often rests on the table rather than in my lap, and I deliberately ignore putting my eyes down when I pass anyone.

Sister Gertrude Marie talked about avoiding particular friendships (PFs was another word in this new culture) in our spiritual talks, having been given continuous warnings that put the fear of God in us. Not only would she emphasize this in many morning lectures, but if she saw two of us huddled together, she would be sure to break us up. Several girls from Long Island were friends before they joined the convent, and it was hard for them to just drop their friendships.

For me, I didn't know anyone, so it would take me some time to form friendships. It took me a long time to figure out that Sister Gertrude Marie was talking about lesbianism. She never mentioned the word. Since I in my short past had valued my friends and was particular about whom I chose for friends, I couldn't quite get why they couldn't be particular. One morning, folding sheets in the laundry with another postulant, she reminded me, "We better be careful we don't get caught talking to each other too often, they will think we are PFs." Finally, I asked her what they were so afraid of. "Lesbianism," she murmured. She was bright, and I thought sophisticated since she was from Manhasset, Long Island, a ritzy community. I wanted to be friends with her. I thought I could break into that Long Island group of early arrivals if she were my friend. That high school thinking did not work in the postulancy.

I didn't even know what the word lesbianism meant, so I looked it up in the dictionary. When I learned they were trying to prevent sexual behavior between two women, the suggestion offended me that they would dare to think I would be interested. Would any of us? After all, chastity was a huge sacrifice giving up that wonderful feeling of being held and kissed by my former boyfriend. Why would anyone join the convent if that were her orientation? I was very naïve. Those girls from Long Island were not.

I had little understanding of human sexuality. What limited amount I knew I had picked up from my friends in high school, but it was mostly about the male homosexual whom we called "sissy." The convent training we experienced provoked us postulants to look with disdain upon the basic desires of some women to love women. Because of the emphasis on "particular friendships," I was not empathetic toward others' inclination to love differently from me in a woman's institution.*

I was thrilled to begin my college education. All of our classes were held in the motherhouse, and they were basic requirements for any freshmen, including theology, philosophy, French, English literature, and math. These classes challenged me, and I delved into the college work with assiduous study. Postulants had no choices except for the few young women who had previously graduated from college. The faculty came to us, assuring that we postulants did not mingle with the college students.

College also brought sports and physical fitness into my life. Most of the other girls had been involved in high school sports like basketball, softball, swimming, lacrosse, and field hockey. I knew how to swim, but that left me out of everything else when they were choosing teams. I do remember joining the synchronized swimming team that gave me a feeling of inclusion.

But often I felt abandoned by my fellow postulants, especially those educated on Long Island in physical education. I felt I did not belong to their clique. They would take over leading our sports games, and none of them ever picked me for a team.

---

* *I understand that the current training of young women in the convent eventually addressed the natural desires of both heterosexual and homosexual women and what chastity meant specifically for everyone. It was not done in my training, and I fear it took me many years to appreciate others' inclinations might be different from mine.*

These girls were the ones who arrived early on entrance day, had the first places in our band, and became a closed group that excluded the rest of us postulants. I recognized I had no familiarity with these games, but I still felt hurt not to be chosen to participate on a team. I swallowed it hard. I experienced the same feeling of humiliation that I did when my mother removed me from the majorettes. Not belonging was mortifying.

I grew to love and respect Sister Gertrude Marie because she took her job of preparing us for this leap into the habit of a nun very seriously while peppering everything with her good sense of humor. But I did not share my humiliation of "not belonging" with her. I felt that she might make an issue of it and then I truly wouldn't have a chance to belong. "Tattling" was not okay with me.

As postulants, we knew that novices had secrets that we were not privy to. Something solemn occurred in the novitiate and the professional nuns' meeting room each Friday night after night prayers. Out of the darkness came the rhythmic chant of many voices undulating for what seemed like hours. We were sure, if this mystery were to be revealed to us, those voices were those of the dead. Was it as occult as it seemed? Was this a witches' coven or a preternatural séance? Why would Sister Gertrude Marie not explain this mystery to us?

Some were brave enough to ask but were told, "in due time." I offered my silence, trusting that these nuns to whom I entrusted my life would not bring harm to me. My bold, questioning self was learning that she did not know everything. I had chosen this new journey and was determined to learn to subjugate my spirit to my superior, despite Uncle Joe's warning.

CHAPTER EIGHT

The Novice Should Never Be Heard

S IX MONTHS OF TRAINING had passed by the time the March winds blew snow and rain throughout the grounds of the motherhouse, and it was our moment to doff our postulant outfits and to take on the habit of the Sisters, Servants of the Immaculate Heart of Mary. *Finally,* I thought, *I will look like a nun.* What would it be like?

We were told that this was the time to dedicate ourselves to be a bride of Christ. I heard these words, "bride of Christ," so often, but I never fully understood the imagery. How many brides could Jesus have? Evidently, as many as He called. I wondered, how was this different from the bigamy in the Mormon church? I was afraid to ask the postulant mistress. So I simply concluded that the church was using this as an image of dedication. My life would be tied to Jesus forever.

Before the solemn ceremony, we donned a white bridal gown and veil and entered the chapel to request to become this bride of Christ. I was uncomfortable with donning this bridal outfit. I felt it was make-believe, a fantasy. I was nervous for my family to see me in this bride's outfit. I couldn't wait to change into the habit.

As we prepared for this solemn day with a 30-day retreat, I focused on what this first year of being a novice was supposed to do: strip me of who I was, my sinful nature. I saw it as a second baptism, but this time it would be a kind of baptism of fire: penance, humiliation, silence, and lots of time to pray. The priest who led our retreat told us as he preached from the altar that this year would demand that we "pray always." Every moment of every day we would dedicate to becoming close to Jesus. We would offer Him our laundry work, our kitchen work, our studies, and our silence. This year was going to be different from anything I had experienced. I wanted to become close to Jesus. So I was ready to become whatever was demanded, even if I had to be called a bride of Christ.

Halfway through the ceremony, we left to change that white gown and veil for a navy blue serge habit and white linen head covering. For the rest of my life, I would have no left or right vision outside these straight horse blinders made of covered plastic. A white veil extending to our waist was the last item to be placed on our heads to signify that we were novices, not yet nuns, who wore the black veil indicating that they had professed their vows. This step indicated that I was truly intending to be a nun. At this moment of transfer, I imagined that I looked like a nun. There were no mirrors.

I had seen my family only once at Christmas. By the time the ceremony in March rolled around, my family saw their formerly very thin teenage daughter and sister waddle down the aisle in a white gown and veil as a bride of Christ. They could not believe this girl was theirs. I had put on 25 pounds in six months! Was I very content with this lifestyle, or was I eating my way through the frustrations of adjusting to convent life? When the ceremony was over, I was unmercifully teased by my brothers, especially Leo. Even though my father tried to act as though he didn't notice that I put on that much weight, I could tell he was holding back. He saw that my face was not happy and that I would try to turn away from the boys who were teasing me. He finally told the boys to cut it out.

I remember that visit was most uncomfortable because, in addition to the teasing, my family continually pressed me to take photos. Even my mother and dad pressured me to pose for them, but I got the strong message from Sister Gertrude Marie that taking my photo was anathema. Later I learned that I took this more seriously than some of the other postulants since they were secretly passing around photos they got undercover.

Somehow I felt my family's insistence on the photos was setting up a distance between them and me. My sister Maureen cried and told me how much she missed me, and it was sad that I would no longer be coming home. But I could not empathize with her. I was happy with my new life. When the visit was over, I was ready to begin my novitiate. I was also highly motivated to lose those pounds. And I did not realize then how easy that would be.

At the end of that very night, we celebrated becoming novices, and our heads were shaved. When I went to my dormitory room, a senior novice stood ready with the shaver. I really didn't want this to happen. I gritted my teeth through these ten minutes. Although there were no mirrors, it took little imagination to experience the loss of my identity, with the emptiness and coldness of a bald head and the piles of dark hair falling to the ground. I understood the purpose was to produce humility. It wasn't until later that I learned that its real purpose was to assure that sweating would be minimal underneath the headgear of plastic covered with white cloth and veil.

On my bedside table lay a rectangular white flannel cloth I was to use to cover my head at night, securing the cloth with a safety pin at the nape of the neck. With my head bent over into the pillow, I tried to hide the tears. Here I was surrounded by white curtains, alone in my single bed with an iron backboard. Yes, it was the Great Silence, but I could hear my sister novices, some coughing, others whimpering, and all lamenting the loss of their hair. We were all unprepared for this ritual. Although I had seen novices in the common bathroom areas at night with these protective covers, I did not suspect that they were bald.

STUDY AND PRAYER

The first year of the novitiate, titled the canonical year and ruled by the Vatican Canon law, was so much more serious than the postulancy. Silence was strictly enforced except for limited times set aside for recreation. It did not take long for me to begin to enjoy the solitude. The rule of "custody of the eyes" was a big help. Eyes never roamed, never looked anyone in their eye, and if mine saw humor, I was supposed to immediately lower them. This was a period where I learned to refrain from any reaction in public. Most of the sisters in my band and I found this very difficult to practice.

These practices and all of our instruction helped us to develop a depth to our spirituality. We studied theology and philosophy under very challenging, but superbly intellectual, professors. Delving into topics of research that dealt with the Church's position on original sin, the Virgin Birth, the Infallibility of the Pope, or the education of Catholic youth fired my intellect. I would search out positions of ancient and modern Church scholars, often finding disagreements. At first, alarmed to find that so many divergences existed among the best scholars in the Catholic Church, it was gratifying to know that everything we were taught in 12 years of religious education was not necessarily fixed or defined doctrine. Plenty of room existed for me to develop my own concepts.

We studied Holy Scriptures with great intensity, and we were often assigned biographies of the saints to read, which I always found fascinating, especially those of women. I admired the sacrifice these saints made in their lives, but imitating them as our novice mistress and my sewing mentor, Sister Emerita, implied we should, was asking too much. The self-flagellations of St. Rose of Lima who burned her arms with hot peppers, or the permanent silence of the cloistered nuns like Catherine of Siena, or the strict asceticism of St. Therese of Lisieux, often known as The Little Flower, were not for me. I was not embracing the temporary silences of the novitiate at first, but eventually I began to understand how silence produced tranquility.

I did enjoy learning to meditate. I recognized the value of prayer and the personal relationship with God that I wanted to develop. My 18-year-old mind was a sponge that could not get enough information about this new life I had chosen.

On the first Friday of the month, we were assigned an hour or more to spend in front of the Blessed Sacrament, which was exposed on the chapel altar in the silver center of this beautiful golden sunburst vessel called a monstrance. Often I filled this time with reading from a spiritual book or saying the rosary. But this one time as I was meditating on what I read, the candles seem to have burst forth with flickering light, and the monstrance seemed so much larger than normal. I was mesmerized. It was a moment of total peace, of pure joy, of ecstasy that seemed to take me out of my body. St. Teresa of Avila claimed to be "one with Jesus" when she wrote of her meditative ecstasies. I was only aware that in some way I had been lifted from tranquility to elation, then rapture, and finally euphoria. This experience was unlike anything I had previously experienced. Many times during the novitiate, I had tried to recreate this experience with little success. I assume that this experience was God's gift to inspire me to continue my dedication to Jesus.

PENANCE

The concept of penance, however, was not something I grasped so easily. Wednesdays and Fridays held secrets unknown to those outside religious life. As a novice, we started each of these mornings with a chainette. This was a metal chain formed like a bracelet with spokes that turned inward on our arm. It was not only uncomfortable, but it often caused bleeding and always left red marks. None of us liked this penance. One time, my arm was infected, and the nurse in the infirmary told me not to wear it for several weeks until she told me I could start again. I hated that chainette, so I welcomed the relief. I also understood that I was not meant for the severe asceticism of the saintly women whose stories we read.

On Friday mornings, we had an exercise which we called "Chapter." Here my stomach would ache and my nerves shudder from the thought of kneeling in front of our entire band of novices as our novice mistress, Mother Adalbert, sat in judgment of all my failings of the week. If I got caught publicly doing something untoward, like breaking the silence or breaking a dish in the kitchen, it better be on my confession list. This was an honor system. Luckily, no one else got to accuse me or anyone else of misbehavior. It reminded me of the weekly confessions of my childhood where Johnny, Maureen, and I made up sins just to satisfy the ritual because, some Fridays, I just made up stuff that I could have done. Maybe I did do these things. I was so nervous, who knows?

What was my greatest penance? The rotating assignment of dining next to Mother Adalbert. I did everything within my power to learn where I was to sit for the week. Each Saturday, I would seek out the novice assigned the task of making sure that each of us had our week of torture. There was no getting out of it. Every novice had to spend a week either to the right or left of the mistress for either breakfast, lunch, or dinner, and those assignments rotated randomly.

Although I never minded that assignment as a postulant with gentle but firm Sister Gertrude Marie, sitting next to Mother Adalbert made me cringe. My stomach knotted, and my nerves twitched as I would try to pick up a glass or a cup. I found it difficult to eat so I would play with my food, which of course brought immediate correction. Learning how to eat to please Mother Adalbert was the surest way for me to lose those 25 pounds.

The novice mistress took her job much too seriously and would correct us for every little thing of which she disapproved. She was new in her job, and we were only her second group of novices. I never got comfortable around her sarcasm, her arrogance, or her corrections. I believed then, and perhaps even now, that she loved too well her job as the prison warden. But I recognized that this was to be my penance of fire. So although I prayed to get out of it, I would end that prayer with "Thy will be done."

Or was flagellation the worst penance? Every Friday after evening prayers and during the Great Silence, all nuns would assemble in a room large enough to hold their community. It might have been the refectory, a recreation room, or even the chapel. For us novices, we met in our large meeting room which we called the novitiate. The lights were out as we assembled and we began the prayer, Psalm 51, Miserere Mei Deus (Have mercy on me, oh God) recited in Latin, followed by the

Psalm 130, De Profundis (Out of the Depths, O Lord). The prayers were accompanied by flagellation. After lifting our skirts, we beat on our bare thighs with a whip as we prayed. This was the secret of the noise we heard on Friday nights as postulants. Yes, our skin got red, and it hurt.

We had to make our own foot-long whip called a discipline, composed of braided rope of several strands folded and tied at the fold and then dipped in wax. This ritual was a scary experience, but penance of any kind was believed to promote the purification of the soul. This concept of physical punishment as a cleansing of the soul sprang from the examples of the saints of the Middle Ages. The belief that self-flagellation or wearing the chainette was a good thing, a Godly act, did not rest well with me. Yet I took the word of our teachers that it was in honor of Jesus' dying on the cross for me, to rescue and to save me from my own originally sinful nature.

We learned that the discipline was commonly used by all religious orders and by pious laity not only in the Catholic Church but also in the Anglican, Lutheran, and Congregational religions. Martin Luther practiced flagellation. We novices knew that we were following an example of the early Christian Church, especially that of St. Paul in memory of Jesus' scourging at the pillar. Yet, most of us didn't like it. I thought it made no sense. Michael Walsh, a Catholic historian, says the practice of flagellation is uncommon today. I hope Walsh is correct, although a writer for Wikipedia claims that flagellation is still practiced in many parts of the world. My fundamental belief about humans is that we need more encouragement of our self-worth and less punishment regarding this ancient belief in our sinful nature.

LEARNING TO OBEY

The novitiate was the time to learn about the meaning of what it meant to take a vow of obedience. We learned that obedience meant to subject ourselves to our superiors. The lessons taught most often meant accepting chores that were humbling. Less penitential than the Friday exercises, the physical labor increased in volume to make up for the time that we no longer spent in college classes during the first year. Peeling potatoes and carrots, washing voluminous pots and pans, setting up dining room table service for more than a hundred nuns, scrubbing and polishing floors, and working in the large commercial laundry were all assigned tasks during this first year of prayer and religious study.

During the second year, our classes expanded to prepare us to be teachers. I became enthusiastic about our college classes, mostly out of fear. Most of us concentrated on elementary education because, at the end of this year, we would be sent out to the missions to stand in front of a classroom filled with 30 or more children and without the normal four years of college to prepare us. I felt frightened and unsure whether I would enjoy teaching.

Another test of accepting the vow of obedience was Mother Adalbert's announcement that I was going to teach piano. Because I had five years of piano lessons (admitting to that was a big mistake), Mother Adalbert informed me that she, herself, would train me to teach piano to fledgling pianists after school. She sat next to me at the piano, took me through exercises, and corrected my bad habits. Each moment of this training felt like punishment. Even in these close encounters, the novice mistress' role was active; she never smiled or showed any empathy. I had no choice. I hoped that when I was sent out to my teaching assignment, the superior would know that I was not qualified to teach piano.

Another test of bending my will to Mother Adalbert was my assignment to help out at St. Joseph's Home, an institution for unwed mothers and orphaned children. My task was to work with the children who had Down syndrome or who were hydrocephalic. Growing up with my young cousin, Mary Ellen, who had Down syndrome made it easier to care for those children and I loved working with them. But the hydrocephalic infants needed such different care. The first time I tried to pick up one child whose head was swollen much larger than his tiny body, I threw up all over the crib. The horrific hospital odor got to my stomach. I had just finished lunch before my assignment. The smells of illness – vomit, sweat, urine, sour milk – and the disinfectant seemed to cling to my habit for days.

I was not only ashamed that deep in my soul I wanted to avoid these children, but I also felt tremendous guilt. I could not understand why these children were alive. They were suffering, and we were working hard to continue their lives. Why? I tried to fight off those feelings, but they clung to me like the stenches on my habit. I felt empathy for the parents who had sent them to this home, but caring for these children demanded more than I could give. I admired the dedication and apparent love that the full-time sister nurses showed to these children. But it was not my calling. Although in high school I had hopes of being a physician, I now knew from this experience that such a career was pure fantasy. I welcomed the opportunity to be a teacher.

A number of our band did not make it to the second year of the novitiate. As our novitiate came to an end in February with its dreary gray skies, its cold Pennsylvania winds, and deep snow covering the landscape, we prepared to take our first vows with 30 days of prayer, silence, and penance. Our retreat was directed by a Redemptorist priest who filled the month with sermons, meditation, and solemnity. I spent much of my free quiet time walking outdoors through the many snow-covered, tree-lined paths on the Marywood campus. Here I found the opportunity to deepen my relationship with Jesus through prayer.

At the end of this retreat, the Mother General and her Council met to determine if we were fit candidates. None of us appeared confident that we would be accepted. I know I wasn't. Mother Adalbert gave me not a hint of which way it would go. I made no plans if I wasn't accepted. I didn't even want to think about the possibility. For two and a half years, we had been pummeled with how we were not worthy to be nuns. We were all reminded how important this Chapter of Request was. The Chapter was an official meeting called for a specific purpose. Would we be accepted into the community and become nuns?

Fearful and trembling, I approached the closed doors of the Chapter meeting room. My hands shook and my stomach ached as I opened the door to face eight women sitting around the very large oak table. Knowing that each of them was ready to discuss my faults and my virtues after Mother Adalbert presented her recommendation shook my body to the bones. I fell on my knees with head and voice lowered, as previously instructed, asking, "I humbly beg to be permitted to make my first vows and to be admitted into the Congregation of the Sisters, Servants of the Immaculate Heart of Mary."

Rumor had it that any one of these nuns could blackball us. Word was that a vote was taken by placing a white or black ball in a jar. One of the last of my band to request this permission, I would not learn until the next day whether I got a yes or a no vote. Mother Adalbert would take each of us individually and convey the verdict. We hung around the hall outside her office to see how our friends made out. Three of our number received the bad news that they were not accepted. No one got to talk to them. They were quietly gone, and none of us knew why. Someone saw one of them packing up and asked where she was going and only got the answer, "Home!"

I was worried; could I be next? By the time my turn came, my nerves felt like they were on fire. Every time we entered the novice mistress' office, she was sitting at her blonde maple desk looking very powerful as we novices knelt on the floor at her side. It felt demeaning, and that was the intent. My heart beat rapidly, and my wet hands were red from wringing them continuously. I entered the office and knelt at the novice mistress' feet.

"Despite your prideful nature, the Council has accepted you. Congratulations."

Any apprehension I had disappeared. Fear turned to anger. She was humiliating me, and I didn't like it. It seemed to give her satisfaction; she did not hide her cynical smile.

Mother Adalbert waited for a response from me. I felt this day was supposed to be a joyous occasion with a celebration planned for that evening, and she had just put a foil in my heart. My 30-day special relationship with Jesus struggled. From down deep came the courage to parry to her lunge: "Didn't you teach us that pride will lead us to the grave? I guess I will be dealing with pride until the day I die." I would no longer bow to her arrogance. Soon she would have no control over me.

March draped the sky in grey, dense clouds and the ground with melting snow dripping through the black cinders of the anthracite area. The weather did not reflect the excitement and joy in my heart when the day of the profession of vows finally arrived. The motherhouse chapel altar was filled with tall, white gladiolas in shining golden vases and the aroma of wax burning brightly in the candelabras. The anxious, glowing faces of parents, siblings, nieces, and nephews plus all our voices rising in harmonious "Gloria" affirmed the solemnity and joy of this moment.

Twenty years old and finally a nun, I floated into the reception hall in my slender body to greet my family with a feeling of having surpassed the sometimes overwhelming demands of the novitiate. I no longer had to worry about my photo being taken, nor was I concerned about pressure to eat with them. My family were guests invited to lunch with us, the first time I had eaten with my family in two and a half years. Three new baby nephews waited to be hugged. My uncle, Father Leo, was a proud attendant with the Bishop. Mother was in her glory, and Dad was Dad. He missed me but it was okay with him. If his kids were happy, he was happy. I no longer had the anxieties of tripping up, doing something wrong for which there would be a confession later along with a punishment by the novice mistress.

This confidence did not last long. Although we were nuns, we had not yet completed our stay in the novitiate. Mother Adalbert, still our superior for the next five months, let us know nothing had changed. Now we were the lowliest of the professed nuns. So, we started all over again on the bottom rung. We still had the same household duties that we had as novices. In addition, we had to get back to completing our classes that were interrupted by the 30-day retreat.

With only two and a half years of college, I felt unprepared for my mission as an elementary school teacher. Student teaching began soon after we professed our vows. The confidence of studying was soon replaced by timidity, doubt, and uncertainty. My nerves unhinged each morning as I headed out for my first try at teaching real sixth-grade students at St. Paul's grade school in Scranton. When the regular teacher was not in the room, they tested my ability to discipline. What was I to do when four boys said they had to go to the boys' bathroom, or the girls started talking?

Those who have experienced student teaching know those feelings of fear: of a room full of children who could instantly take over if you let them; of the supervising teacher telling you how awful your teaching was; or of the principal declaring you were no longer acceptable in her school. These things never materialized, but this didn't stop my mind from running wild that it might. When June came, we had two summer sessions to give us as much preparation as possible. Yet confidence still escaped my grasp.

CHAPTER NINE

A Teaching Voice is Learned

WAITING FOR THE TEACHING ASSIGNMENTS to be announced kept us anxious and excited. I prayed that I would be sent out far beyond the bounds of Pennsylvania. I got my wish. My assignment was to St. Raymond's School in East Rockaway, Long Island. The pressure was on when Mother Adalbert explained that this was a challenging assignment. "You will need to be at your best in this school. The parents of those children care about their education." I did not have a college degree, and I was going to be teaching sixth graders in an uppity school? Why assign me? But one did not question an assignment, especially to Mother Adalbert.

St. Raymond's proved to be a very lucky assignment for me. Sister Marie Thomas, the superior of the convent and the principal of the school, took me under her wing, training me, prodding me, challenging me to become a good teacher. Sister guided me in my preparation each Sunday afternoon, helping me to write my lesson plans for the week, challenging me to create exercises that would interest the class, checking the homework assignments I gave. Few first-year teachers in Catholic or public schools, with or without a college degree, got the attention and assistance that my principal provided me.

Marie Thomas challenged me to create my first test in history by myself. I failed miserably because every student but one in the sixth-grade class did not pass. For the most part, these were very bright students. The students failed because of the way I structured the questions. I trashed the tests without giving the students any results. But they pestered me until finally I told them they did so poorly that they would have another chance. This time I had learned from my mistakes.

It was humiliating, however, to admit to Marie Thomas that the history test was a disaster, and I waited a week until I could eat that humble pie.

Another source of support, Sister Gonzales, my co-teacher of the sixth grade, 65 years old and teaching for nearly 50 years, decided that my penmanship was a disaster. And so she taught me Palmer Method every night after dinner until my penmanship improved sufficiently to be a worthy teacher in her community. Have you ever wondered why sisters had such good penmanship? Now you know; we had lessons and lots and lots of practice.

Gonzales often seemed irritated that Marie Thomas, my superior and my principal, took over my training and didn't assign her the job of being my mentor. Because Gonzales and I were teaching the same material, I would try to engage her in discussing how she taught the lesson. Often rebuffed, I sensed that she felt hurt and maybe envious, making sly remarks about my class and telling me that I "evidently was smart enough to figure it out on my own." That motivated me even more to pursue her help until she willingly shared her knowledge and teaching skills. I needed to learn as much as I could from her and get her on my side.

Great credit goes to these two women who took me under their wings, determined to make me not only love teaching but become good at it. After I left East Rockaway, I did not see or hear from them. I wonder why we never connected. I certainly never tried, but neither did they. They have both passed on, and I hope that at some time they knew how they impacted my life as a teacher.

I spent only one year teaching sixth grade and moved on from working with Gonzales, but not from benefitting from her achievements with the seventh-grade students I inherited the next year. These bright kids were a challenge to me. Margaret Coogan, an identical twin with a derisive laugh, corrected me for mispronouncing Wolfgang as in Mozart. "The W in German, Sister, is pronounced like a V. Everybody knows that." Four years of French and Latin in high school and two semesters of French in college were not sufficient to deal with this 13-year-old Coogan.

Several incidents such as this reminded me of how little background I had. To my chagrin, caught red-handed by my education superintendent, Sister Felicitas, who was evaluating my teaching, I misidentified ebony in a geography lesson. Margaret corrected me and made it clear that it was a beautiful South American wood. I knew it was black, but I thought it was coal — Margaret Coogan should have been teaching the class. I came from the very black coal anthracite region which definitely was not "the" ebony but still an ebony color. Sister Felicitas did not let me live this down as she joined us for dinner that evening.

When I taught eighth grade in 1960, the young teenage girls were shocked that I did not know who the Beatles were. So these Beatle fans brought their boom-box to outdoor recess and played the songs. I caught on to the beat and loved it. Adding to my repertoire of '60s music, another set of twins, Meg and Beth Schratweiser, insisted I learn how to dance the Mashed Potato and the Twist. I mashed and twisted as other students gathered to cheer me on. Six yards of blue habit hiked up about my knees was difficult, but I danced on with the twins, never aware that other nuns were observing this un-nun-like behavior. Dancing was always my thing, and learning what the world was obsessed with thrilled my starving soul. Not so thrilling was the older nuns telling the story to embarrass me at the dinner table that night. Someone was looking out the convent window at noon, and this made great fodder.

Teaching 30 students for seven hours a day, and then four students each a half-hour of piano every evening along with college classes on Saturday, showed its punishment more than once. As I sat at the piano teaching a student, I would catch myself nodding, trying to stay awake. My student nudged me, "Sister, Sister, are you okay?" Startled, I awoke. She found me asleep, so I had to admit with apology to this 12-year-old that I was tired. To this day, I blame drinking milk at lunch. So from then on, I drank tea or coffee and there was no falling asleep, although my head did bob.

I loved the children and their energy, curiosity, and warm encounters with me both in the classroom and on the playground. I believe that it was my love of teaching these children that motivated my life as a nun. I would look forward every day to greeting the children and nurturing their eager minds. I was not so happy when school was out in the summer. I looked forward to taking classes so I could get my degree, but studying was not as satisfying, or as much fun, as teaching.

One unhappy memory was the summer of 1962 after my fourth year of teaching. Marie Thomas announced that I was not going to attend classes that summer. Rather than continue my studies, I was assigned as a housekeeper for one of our convents. They needed young energy to share the work of caring for the house. At that point, I had spent seven years and still held no degree. I was angry, disappointed, and frustrated that I was wasting this summer. I made my case to her but to no use. "It is God's will," she reminded me.

When I talked to Jesus in prayer, I asked, "Was this really your will, Jesus?" I got no answers. The superior at this summer convent was my superior's best buddy. They cooked up this assignment together. That superior breathed a cold arrogance and snobbishness that made her unlikeable. Those two dear buddies enjoyed many creature comforts that the rest of us had no access to: Broadway plays, alcohol, weekends away, several-week vacations at the shore, friendships with the wealthy parishioners and family members. All of this scandalized me because of what I considered their disregard for the vow of poverty. I was young, idealistic, and naive. I believed in my vows, so why didn't they act like they believed in theirs?

One nun, at least 15 years my senior who remained in the convent that summer, developed a crush on me. She wanted me to reciprocate by attending events with her. She arranged the schedule so we would be preparing dinner together or scrubbing the refectory. The way she looked at me made me very uncomfortable. My skin would grow cold if I even had to stand next to her. I avoided her whenever I could. But we two were the only physically capable nuns assigned to that convent for the summer. We would often have strangers visiting, using the convent as their room and board, so I was kept busy doing laundry, changing sheets, and sweeping floors.

One day she told me I was to accompany her on about a 90-minute drive out of the city. A parishioner let her know that he had an errand up there and asked if she wanted to ride along to visit her friends at our convent in the area. So as we sat in the back seat, she tried to touch me and hold my hand, which I rejected by pulling away from her. My skin felt like bugs were crawling up those wide habit sleeves. She persisted by whispering nonsense in my ear, disgusting and intimidating me. I immediately moved as far to the other side of the car that I could. She looked at me, and I saw her face was flushed. I felt she was making a scene, and the driver was going to notice if I didn't do something. I could tell he sensed some tension in the back seat.

I moved forward in the car to engage our driver as though nothing was happening. The parishioner-driver was doing my companion a favor. I started a conversation to interact with him. "Do you have children in school? What grades are they? What are they doing for the summer?" I continued that mode until we reached our destination. Finally, as we were walking toward the convent door, I found the voice I did not know I had.

"Why would you think that it was okay to touch me in that car? How could you humiliate me like that? Do not ever try anything like that again!"

She turned red and whispered as she turned away from me, "I don't know what you are talking about." She was quite silent on our ride back to the convent, but I dreaded that ride and every day after.

Most upsetting was that I had to live with this nun for another month as my temporary superior. Each day was an effort to escape her presence. She never apologized or attempted to touch me again, but I lived with the fear of what she might report to her superior. Would she make up a story to get ahead of what I might do?

Why did I not report this scene to my superior? I was scared of her response. Would she ridicule me? Not believe me? Deny that it was even possible? I felt strongly that neither superior would have believed me over the older sister's story or defense. I wonder, if I were alert then to what I know now, would I have reported the incidents? I don't believe I would have taken that risk. In our "Me too" culture, women have shown the courage to report unwelcome incidences. Whenever I hear of a woman's rights to her own body being violated, I empathize with her humiliation, guilt, fear of being doubted, and hesitancy to act. More than anything, I admire her courage to speak up.

I did not understand lesbianism as a natural feeling. And I had no empathy for women who were attracted to women. I did not understand that it was simply another way of loving another. Homosexuality was not accepted by the Church then, and officially not even today. I believed in the Church's rules then. I also believed in my vow of chastity. I never doubted the sacredness of what I believed and how I expected it to be practiced. Today I am chagrined that I was so ignorant of the natural feelings of one's attraction to one of the same gender.

The summer passed and I was happy to get back to the opening of school. Someone at the motherhouse must have put the pressure on my superior to get me through school because the next two years were packed with classes. In the fall, I began two Saturday classes in English literature at St. John's University in Jamaica.

CHAPTER TEN

I Find My Voice

I FELT LIKE CELEBRATING, AND I DID. My parents came to the graduation and held a party at their home for me. Seven years of part-time study after the novitiate seemed like an eternity. But having that diploma in my hand gave me a sense of achievement.

When I learned that my new assignment was teaching English to high school students, I was excited. The fact that the school, St. Rose, was located in Carbondale, Pennsylvania, on top of an underground burning mine that exuded sulfur and other gases did not dissuade me. I had heard that the principal, Sister Rebecca, was hard on young sisters and that she had her favorites. Those six years with Sister Marie Thomas gave me the courage to go forward with my vocation. Perhaps I became more realistic about the humanity of my religious sisters.

Even after my first year of teaching high school, my superior-principal gave me no quarter. Since I was the youngest again, Sister Rebecca piled on me the tasks of running the kitchen, preparing the menus for the cook, buying the groceries, and preparing lunches to be taken to the school for 16 nuns. Sometimes those duties conflicted with my teaching responsibilities. It was hard to manage my time.

My school schedule that first year was very full, teaching freshmen and sophomore English for seven periods. I was pumped, except for one class. I was scheduled to teach the less-than-genius sophomore English group during the last period each afternoon. By this time of day for any teacher, one's energy is drained. Those students were not intellectually dull; many of them "dumbed down" because their parents, exhausted, gave up on them. Or teachers who had 30 or more students in their classes had to let them slide. Teaching children who take more time to learn is a challenge, especially to keep their attention.

Ironically, the class that I eventually looked forward to the most was this group of students. Teaching English literature to these kids turned out to be fun because there was plenty of creativity in this group. When we studied ballads, they brought their guitars, and we sang like the troubadours of the Renaissance. When it was time for poetry, we wrote songs imitating the masters or capitalizing on the students' talents. I resigned myself that these students were not going to go on to college, or whatever they wanted to do in life, unless they gained confidence that they were capable of learning. Some were not as capable as others, but the last period of the day was no longer a burden to them or me.

One student from this class submitted a poem to a national poetry magazine for high school students, and he won first prize in his category. This award brought recognition to him when the principal announced the award over the broadcast system in the school. He could hear the raucous applause and whistles coming from all the students. His classmates cried, "Hurray for us!" They took on his praise as their own. All the sophomores had written poems for the contest, but one of them winning over all the "smart" kids was reason for celebration. I followed these sophomore students the next year into junior English and American literature, the forensics club, and the literary quarterly. We had bonded.

In my last year of teaching, one of these students faced me with a question about two nuns. "Are (so and so) lesbians?" Gasping for air, I had not heard the word lesbian since the novitiate; I wondered if I heard him correctly. He began to describe discovering them hand in hand on a walk. Embarrassed by his question, I tried to play down what he saw.

"Sister, I know what I saw. They look like lovers to us. Ask Kathy, she was with me. This isn't the first time. We're not blind. We see this stuff."

Further humiliated when he scolded me for shutting my eyes to the relationship, I felt I had to do something about this. After a few days of cowering, I finally gathered my courage and told Sister Rebecca, our superior-principal, about the scuttlebutt among the kids. As I expected, she blamed the messengers,

"You know how teenagers are. They let their imaginations go wild and make up stories."

I finally knew why the novice mistress continually stressed the dangers of "particular" friendships. But my thoughts were those of my novice mistress. It was wrong. These kids were scandalized. Teenagers pick up hypocrisy very quickly. They were judging what we said we stood for. The vow of chastity required abstinence whether it be homosexuality or heterosexuality.

But what effect did this emphasis on "particular" friendships have on me? And on how many others of us nuns? At this point I had been in the convent for ten years, and I was prompted to examine why I had no friendships. I had no nuns with whom I felt close. Yet I was aware of many friendships of other nuns that seemed supportive and close. I did not envy them or judge them. I did not feel lonely. I was excited about my work. Then I remembered that one summer as the housekeeper in New York when I wished I had someone in whom I could confide. Perhaps, I thought, I'm just a loner.

During the summer between these two years in Carbondale, I studied at Notre Dame for my masters. One of my teachers, Richard Poorman, a Holy Cross priest, asked me if I would consider going on for a doctorate. He indicated that there would be a scholarship available for me, and he would write the Mother General of my community requesting that I be released for study. I really didn't believe that she would allow me to go on for the doctorate. No one had ever mentioned anything about going on beyond the masters in the past. When I met with the Mother General, she was open and eager about the offer. She apologized to me for having to delay my going to Notre Dame for a year since teaching assignments had already been made. Nevertheless, I was thrilled to think that I, Aggie Jordan from West Pittston, Pennsylvania, would be a doctoral student at the University of Notre Dame. Would my parents think that I had hit the jackpot?

When Sister Rebecca was told of the decision, she requested that we keep this news quiet. Disappointed that I could not share this joy with anyone, I still had to act as though nothing was going on for the remaining eight months. I couldn't even tell my family. I knew they wouldn't be able to keep it a secret. They would be so proud and want to tell all the friends and relatives.

In early September, the beginning of this last year at St. Rose, the school semester became overloaded with a full schedule of classes, producing the literary quarterly, and training students interested in forensic competition. At the same time, a parishioner-farmer offered Sr. Rebecca the opportunity to pick the fall surplus of their tomatoes. Rebecca was in her glory. When she was in Coeur d'Alene, Idaho, as the superior, she ran a farm for the Academy, and she loved it. Rebecca was a ruddy-faced, rotund, five-foot-tall lover of all things farming. This call to collect tomatoes gave her a thrill.

"We have to pick as many tomatoes as we can and move them into the baskets for transport. It's a big job, and I need as many people as I can get to come with me."

I was happy it was not an order. She was asking for volunteers. I did not volunteer to pick "stupid tomatoes" even though kitchen management was my job. We were having forensic competitions during the following two weekends for the students, and it was my immediate task to prepare them. My decision got some angry looks from Rebecca's cache of favorites. When they returned with 20 bushels of tomatoes, I resisted the pressure to begin the canning process. But those nuns who picked, piled, and packed those baskets into the parishioners' trucks followed Rebecca into the kitchen and cooked, bottled, and stored hundreds of jars of tomatoes. I stayed in school and prepared the students for the local contests.

Tomatoes became an item on the daily menus. Eventually the nuns asked for a reprieve. By the late spring, we had enough tomatoes for the next year, but Rebecca decided to give me an order: "Make sure you use up all those tomatoes before we leave for the summer. We'll be getting more in the fall."

I went to the cellar and counted the jars that were left. I couldn't believe it. Rebecca repeated the order several times until finally, I answered, "I'll do what I can, but there's no way we can eat 50 jars of tomatoes in four weeks." This tomato incident, as ludicrous as it may sound, appeared to give me the confidence to stand up to her instead of bowing to the ridiculous. Testing me many times during the year with her bullying tactics, I found Rebecca only needed resistance. Finally, I had some control, but I was never accepted into her heart nor she into mine.

The news of my leaving for Notre Dame leaked out. Envy seemed to rear its ugly head when some of the sisters learned what was in my future. I'm sure it was Rebecca who couldn't keep it quiet and shared with her favorites. Sarcasm crept into the conversation, and I experienced the separation from the community a month before I left. Was this the beginning of my path out?

CHAPTER ELEVEN

I Find Myself

I N THE AUTUMN OF 1966, I schlepped my suitcase into a taxi at the
South Bend Airport bound for a newly constructed Lewis Hall on the
shores of St. Mary's and St. Joseph's lakes, which had opened its doors
to women graduate students that fall, the first females to have a home
on the Notre Dame campus. To be a resident in this beautiful setting
with women, predominantly nuns, thrilled me.

Amid Vietnam protests, folk music, and draft card burnings, I
landed at Notre Dame in a blue serge habit, a white wimple, and a
headdress of white horse blinders masked with a black veil. The covering
provided me with solid security from the university's unknown world.
Concealed in the habit, I felt secure but often invisible.

My first task after settling in was to search out Professor Poorman
to express my gratitude for his initial efforts in getting me to the university. He was nowhere to be found. His whereabouts appeared to be a
secret. It took a week before I learned from my department chair that
Poorman had left the priesthood. The sixties were breaking through
all kinds of barriers, but proscriptions still existed about "scandals" of
priests or nuns leaving.

I could not easily accept the irony of Professor Poorman's influence
on my being there while he was not. For a short time, I sensed a deep
loss and felt abandoned. I asked a couple of my professors if they knew
how I could reach him, but they had no information. "I'm afraid he left
quietly," said one. And another mentioned, "We never got a chance to
say goodbye." A few years later I learned of his death.

As the fall semester got underway, everything seemed to be a
turn-on: the challenge of graduate studies, finding my way around

the campus, the intellectual atmosphere, making new friends, the excitement of the campus protests, the deep spirituality that suffused everything we did, and of course, the excitement of Notre Dame football. I was a football fan from my high school days when I wanted to perform as a majorette with the band on the football field.

Meeting my new fellow students, engaging in the class discussions and the intellectual give-and-take among my colleagues at Lewis Hall, I was thriving. In our classes, we delved into the History of Education in a seminar where about eight of us listened to the expert, Dr. Kohlbrenner. Fr. Neil McCluskey, S.J., an internationally known expert in the field of Catholic education, was our professor in the Philosophy of Education. The influence of both of these educators, among many others, inspired us — particularly because of the time they spent with us outside class. We never knew when one of them would drop in on our group work and invite us to their home for a burger and a beer.

The life-changing process I experienced involved more than being enrolled in a Ph.D. program with the classes; the research, the intellectual challenge, the hours spent in a library carrel, or even the professors at Notre Dame who were very connected with each graduate student. No longer was I invisible. The seed was planted by my relationships with my hallmates. These sisters from communities across the nation engaged me in multiple philosophical discussions as we sat and shared breakfast, lunch, or dinner in our third-floor kitchen in Lewis Hall.

Conversation among all Catholics in the late 1960s, particularly among those who had dedicated their lives to the Catholic Church, centered on the windows that Pope John XXIII had opened for us to allow fresh air in. No question went unasked because of fear or critical judgment of others. I found an atmosphere of acceptance that was not present in my community back in Carbondale. I learned to love these dear women, who were also learning to live with new guidelines alongside the old, fixed rules. They infused in me the spirit of feminism. I became aware that women were not treated equally anywhere — in the university, in the family, in the government, or even in the Church.

Marilyn Hofer, a Franciscan sister from Terre Haute, Indiana, a woman of great simplicity and exceptional intelligence, joined me as the only other woman admitted to the Ph.D. program in Education. She also was sent by her community to prepare to become a dean or president of her college. We became dependent on each other for support because the department chair and some of the professors viewed the male students, cleric and lay alike, as the ones who would attain the jobs of greater responsibility. No doubt, the University of Notre Dame celebrated males. Marilyn and I were never sure if this subtle exclusion was because we were women or because we were nuns. We fought to be heard. Eventually we claimed our place among the students who had the potential to make it.

The work challenged my physical and intellectual capacities. One of the perks of this program was that we were assigned our individual carrels in the new library. I loved the privacy of this 5'x 6' space where I spent ten to 12 hours a day as the towering "Touchdown Jesus" mural spanned the height and width of the library structure on the outside wall facing the football stadium. This depiction of Jesus with his hands in the air became the landmark that enabled me to find my way around campus.

Another dear friend who helped me to plot my course through the doctorate was a fellow student, Roger Parent, a former Peace Corps volunteer in Thailand, married and the father of three children. Roger and I took most of the same classes and studied together for the first two years of the program. A politician (who eventually became Mayor of South Bend) with a dedication to community service, Roger introduced me to volunteering with the Neighborhood Study Help Program, a direct service for mentoring marginal students in the South Bend area. Notre Dame supported the program with volunteer students, and Roger as the Director of the Community Service ran it. The students were from poor families, and naively I thought that all the poor could be counted on to keep the rules of honesty. My family, particularly my mother and dad, were always involved in community service and causes for social justice.

I had to learn the hard way that keeping any cash on me was a bad idea. Because I was living on a pittance from month to month, I could not afford to be careless with my money. When my month's allowance was stolen from my purse by one of the children, I suffered. Telling the story to Roger got me no sympathy.

"What? Are you nuts? Of course, some of those kids will steal, they need the money. They're poor. You need to be careful."

Roger saw the need to educate me as much as he could, including why I should learn to drink scotch. At parties, I would not drink alcohol because the sweet drinks made me ill. At a party at his house, Roger handed me a glass of Dewar's and said, "Sip on it slowly. You'll get used to it, and it won't make you sick." No doubt it was his way of telling me to loosen up. Scotch has been my drink of choice ever since, but now it's Johnnie Walker Black.

A friendship that has survived my years since my time at ND is with Mary Margaret Zanglein Singer Dickinson. Mary Marg was my bulwark of love, compassion, peace, joy, and comic relief. A sister IHM from the congregation in Monroe, Michigan, she brought a brightness to my life beginning in my third year and every year since. Mary Marg's mother was Irish Catholic, and her father was German Lutheran. This combination seemed to free her from the "religious fever" of my Irish family. Perhaps this freedom was strengthened by her time at Fordham University seeking her master's degree in psychology before she joined those Michigan IHM's.

Mary Marg's spirit of *joie de vivre* treated the demimonde or the sacred with the same lack of gravitas. Yet her humor, her intellectual genius, and her generous, warm heart drew her a circle of friends immediately. She demonstrated the difference between those of us who joined the convent before we had any idea of adulthood and reality, compared to one who had matured with a good dose of common sense.

Suzanne, a friend of Mary Marg's from the same Monroe IHMs, had total disregard for the rules. An artist of Andy Warhol's taste and talent, Suzanne seemed to step on the sacred whether it appeared ridiculous or important. I admired these two nuns, sharing the same community rules as me, but recognizing that life was not as serious as I thought. These women opened my eyes to the joy that I had missed in my previous time in the convent.

As the sun rose over St. Joseph's Lake, I excitedly greeted each day and the challenges of study it presented. But the moment I waited for at the end of each day was the midnight Mass in Farrell, Sorin, or Walsh Halls. Gathering with the students of every class, freshmen to seniors, plus graduates in engineering, law, science, or sociology, awakened me to the world as I did not know it. The Holy Cross fathers designed the liturgy for participation. We stood around the altar and engaged in a discussion led by the presiding priest at homily time. We were nourished by each other and the presence of two or three gathered in Christ's name. It is this experience that continues to remind me of what the Catholic Church can be. I miss this community experience today and find myself continuing to seek it out. But I have not been successful in my search for a Catholic Church that offers support. I find my spirituality strengthened by my friends who are Catholic and also by those who have their own belief systems different from mine.

One lesson I did learn from a few of my Lewis Hall mates was the importance of physical exercise in handling stress. Each morning, a number of us would put on our walking or running shoes and head for a trek around St. Mary's lake. Whether rain or snow pelted the ground, or the sun shined through the trees warming my face, I felt pleasure in the solitude, in the cold air, in getting my mind organized for the day, a habit I have carried through to this day. Exercise was the initiator of shedding the habit.

To make this exercise simple, I had to shop. Running or walking in the habit and oxford shoes was not okay. So off I went with Mary and Germaine Gilbert, two Sisters of Loretto from Aurora, Colorado, who had been freed from the habit before they came to Notre Dame. Eleven years had passed since I had purchased clothes for myself. We scoured the thrift shops for sports clothes and running shoes. South Bend demanded snug jackets and cozy wool hats, warm gloves, grey jogging sweatpants, and lots of hot coffee in the winter. What I couldn't find was something to cover my eyelashes so they would not stick together with blowing snow. But the summers were perfect. I was not brave enough to buy shorts the first two years. Finally, in my third year, I gained the confidence that running shorts were fine.

Mary and Germaine Gilbert proved to be good friends during my second year. In their early twenties, they were both studying for a master's in religious education. These two women, bursting with energy, were totally tuned in to whomever they spoke to. Breaking out in laughter, eyes shining with glee, they were magnetic.

As Easter approached in 1968, I headed to California to do my research on the Claremont Colleges, one of the subjects for my dissertation on consortiums of higher education. The Gilbert sisters invited me to join them as they headed home to Colorado for the spring holiday. They asked me to stay at their home for a few days. Germaine had her own reasons for wanting me. She needed to break the news to her parents that she planned to leave the convent in May and marry a priest she had fallen in love with at the high school where they previously taught. If I were there with them, Germaine shared, any negative reaction to her news would be lessened.

Her sister Mary and I took off for beautiful Estes Park to give Germaine the privacy she needed to talk to her mother. Germaine, excited and thrilled at her choice, and Mary totally supportive, had to face the reality that their mother was not ready for their oldest daughter to leave the convent and marry a priest.

In Catholic families at the end of the 1960s, this scenario became more frequent. Lives were changing as the rules we lived by began to disappear. This flummoxed me to a point where I began to understand that life was not as simple as my naive existence understood.

I was happy at Notre Dame because of the fond friendships I was able to develop. It was the dear friends at Lewis Hall who allowed me to grasp the importance of having attachments. It taught me to seek out friends wherever life took me.

On Easter Monday, I joined another nun who lived in Colorado and had a car. We drove the rest of the near 1,000 miles to Claremont, California.

CHAPTER TWELVE

The Women's Movement: My Awakening

WHERE WAS I IN 1963 when women heard the first roar of Betty Friedan in her book, *The Feminine Mystique*? I'm not sure that there was anyone in my convent in East Rockaway, New York, who spoke of this call to women's liberation in America. Certainly not in Carbondale, Pennsylvania. The only conversation I remember was the disdain the other nuns expressed for Ms. Friedan. Many nuns, including me, accepted the Church's culture that we were subservient to men. Because we had given our lives to the Church, did we feel threatened by women's liberation?

Before I arrived at Notre Dame, I knew very little about the women's movement. Sure, I had enough to do as a high school English teacher, a kitchen manager for a convent with 15 or more nuns, and preparations for graduate school. There just wasn't extra time for other readings or outside interests. I am embarrassed now and ashamed that my ignorance deprived me of discussing this major movement with my high school students. No doubt it was of interest to the junior and senior young women who were preparing for their futures. And I failed them.

Before this period, women were generally expected to have a limited number of roles in society: marriage and motherhood, "old maid" teachers, nurses, secretaries, and clerks. Many women got married right out of high school and others within a couple of years of graduating. Few expectations existed for women to have a career.

Although women operated hair salons, childcare, housecleaning, and other businesses that catered to women's needs, individual women who sought success in medicine, law, and business had little support, especially if they were married. Women in the United States and other western countries had a very long trek to achieve any kind of equality until the feminist women came along in the sixties.

For me, the '60s presented another major change. Pope John XXIII called for a Vatican Council that would, he hoped, open the doors for the Church to become more relevant. These two social movements of feminism and the Vatican Council merged at Notre Dame. For me, these two movements were life-changing. I feel they were the propellant for me to leave the convent.

The theology department at Notre Dame invited a widely known male scholar from Germany to speak on campus. He would address the changes that were going on in the Council and the role of women in the Church. I enjoyed the lecture until I arrived back at Lewis Hall. There, a heavy discussion was in process with an overflowing crowd of lay and religious women in the large room off the lobby. The theologian called women the receptacles in the Church, using the vagina analogy, and the men, the action-makers. That was true as I saw the Catholic Church. I snuck into the back of the room and heard this emotional outcry,

"We may have vaginas, but we are not receptacles for every part of our lives." The leader of this very passionate group was arousing great support. I listened intently to Sister Suzanne, a Ph.D. professor of Theology, and she made a lot of sense. By the end of that discussion, I had changed. From the nun who accepted herself as a receptacle in the Church, subservient to priests and bishops, obedient to her superiors, I began to question my life as a nun. How much had I been taking for granted? So, being smart enough to go to Notre Dame, how could I be so stupid, so blind to accept all this nonsense the Church wanted us to believe about women in general and nuns in particular? This moment was like I had been hit with lightning. The brightness of a different reality, the fire of anger at myself, at the Church, the burnt earth of my life. What had I been doing? I certainly had not been using my brain for questioning like these women in this room were. Did all these women understand the importance of women's rights in their lives?

Conversation after conversation at the breakfast table in Lewis Hall or walking across campus to the library with my sisters proved that I was not alone. Women's lack of equality punched us in the gut. We were not equal, and we better do something about it. This was the first time I had grasped the relationship of the Vatican Council to the importance of feminism in every aspect of the Church. Here was the possible fulfillment of my teenage dream to have women priests. I knew God approved of this women's movement because She made us into her image and likeness. Besides, God was intelligent. The movement within the Catholic Church to bring it up-to-date and the women's movement made sense.

This discussion planted the seed that the fight for women's equality was one I would be dedicated to. The irony was that I was indeed the receptacle for that seed, and it would grow in me. I read every article on women's issues that I could get my hands on in the library, and they were in abundance. I attended theological lectures that seemed to be overflowing into the halls with students, male and female, who questioned the place of women in the Church. Many of those women were interlopers from St. Mary's College.

In addition, women would bring up these issues during homilies at late night Mass. Notre Dame was engaged with becoming co-educational. The atmosphere was electric, and I participated in everything that dealt with being female and action-oriented. Somehow all this evolved into my becoming a Catholic feminist and a firm believer in expanding the role of women. I wanted me and all women to become who we longed to be. Could I do this as a nun? As a member of my community in Scranton, Pennsylvania?

RESEARCH AT THE CLAREMONT COLLEGES

One month at the Claremont Colleges provided me the opportunity to wet my feet in this newfound assurance that I counted as a woman. I became a new woman. I felt confident that I was free to explore. The faculty and staff at the Claremont Graduate School were most gracious in providing me with the information I needed and in making me comfortable. Their hospitality was beyond measure. They even provided me with my first helicopter ride to the Los Angeles airport from Pasadena. But I was lonely. I missed my friends at Notre Dame. I did not miss anyone in my home community. Could I bring this spirit back to them? Would it flourish there?

This month at Claremont proved my ability to function totally on my own, away from the university and my religious community. I had spent many days in 1968 with the Associated Colleges of the Midwest (ACM) in Chicago. I also visited the presidents of the "Big Ten" universities, interviewing them for my research on consortiums, using daily trips from Notre Dame to complete my work. But those visits were not as freeing as that time at Claremont.

A STINT AT COLUMBIA

Dr. James Michael Lee, our Chair, suggested that, because my community and I were interested in preparing me for an administrative role at the college, I should take some classes in higher education at Columbia University in New York City. Columbia University School of Education had one of the few and the best-known curricula in higher education. With the permission of my Mother General, I enrolled at Columbia for two summer sessions. We had two convents in the city, and I chose to stay at the convent on Thompson Street, even though this would involve a long subway ride to 120th Street. The two months during the summer that I had spent at the convent on 33rd Street were still a bitter memory.

Sister Mary Evans, a Dominican from Rosary College in Illinois, heard of my plans to spend the summer in New York City and saw an opportunity to join me while she did her research in the Metropolitan Art Museum. Mary was in her full Dominican habit, with flowing long white robes, long scapular, and full headdress. The Dominican sisters were slow to make their changes. But Mary's red face, radiating blue eyes, and bubbly personality burst through all that garb. She was an exciting woman, brilliant, and as open as any of the sisters in Lewis

Hall. I believed the sisters in that convent would love her. So I inquired if the sisters had room for her, and with the permission of my Mother General, we made arrangements for Mary to join me.

During the preceding year, my community of sisters were responding to the call of Rome to update our Rules. They sent out requests for proposals. During this year, I had up-to-date information on a large number of communities that had changed out of the habit into normal, acceptable secular clothes. I suggested keeping a uniform look but adding a much more contemporary dress for our habit. My proposal was far distant from the proposal of my friends who advocated secular dress.

I included some other ideas about spending more time with family and some freedom of choice in our assignments. I submitted the text to the committee responsible for proposals, and they distributed it to all the convents. The proposals had arrived in the mail shortly before Mary Evans and I hit their doorstep with our suitcases.

We did not receive a warm welcome. The sisters had previously fully discussed my proposal, and they were livid. They felt attacked by the concept of change, and they attacked me personally. "That's what happens when you send them to Notre Dame," said one senior sister. Another said, "How could you do this to us?" I wasn't sure I did anything but submit a proposal. It was my "thinking" she didn't understand or approve of. I tottered between nervousness and anger. I tried to explain what was happening in the communities across America, but the rebuttal got angrier. "You are throwing out God. Our habits say we are dedicated to Him. How can you betray us like that?"

Mary Evans felt the tension and wondered if she should have been there at all. Her presence did not seem to make an impact on the nuns. Their usual generous hospitality was thrown out that window that Pope John XXIII had opened.

I addressed the issue with the superior. She was strongly on the side of no change. I tried to explain that it was only a proposal. My suggested innovative dress was getting many positive reviews throughout the community, but not there. Their fear of change was shouting at me to be heard. Mary was there for a month, but I had to endure eight weeks of living with this hell that had broken loose. The revolution and evolution were full blown.

For the most part, the sisters would not speak to either of us at the dinner table in the evening. On the weekends, Mary went back to her research at the museum, and I stayed in my room, skipping community meals whenever it was possible. Although Mary and I thought their behavior was nasty and incredible for people who claimed to follow Jesus and His commandment to love one another, after the first day or two, we did not confront any of them. The atmosphere was bad enough without confrontation.

After I completed my studies at Columbia, I spent the remaining two weeks between a retreat at our motherhouse in Scranton and some days with my family. This brought my vocation back into balance because I had valuable discussions with some of the nuns who were much more open to change. I returned to Notre Dame with permission to wear the new habit as an experiment. During the third year, because of the travel I did with my dissertation research, I converted to a secular dress.

CHAPTER THIRTEEN

Change Your Clothes.
Change Your Life.

I WAS IN THE MIDST OF MAJOR CHAOS at Notre Dame. It seemed that changing one's habit should not be a big deal. Should we be that concerned about what we wear? There were issues bigger than clothes.

Young theologians dared to present ideas previously anathema: the importance of birth control, denying the infallibility of the Pope, the importance of engaging Third World peoples in new theology, women and married priests, lay ministers of the Eucharist, teachers of catechetical students. Some of these theologians remained in the Church as priests; others found a new path when the Church refused to move. Because their leadership was so strong and right, others followed.

The issues of the vows of poverty, chastity, and obedience were called into question for many of the people I admired. My mentor, a Holy Cross father, was leaving the priesthood and getting married. So many of my friends who I had spent the last four years with were leaving and getting married. Lectures and discussions about these vows prevailed throughout the campus. I had questions.

Was I really living the life of poverty that I thought Jesus was teaching? True, I didn't own anything, yet my financial wellbeing for the last four years was provided by a Notre Dame fellowship. Except for the first semester when my community paid for room and board, my own religious community had no financial responsibility for me. I was responsible. Poorer than I had been when living in a community where all my needs were taken care of, I understood more personally the meaning of the vow of poverty in a deeper sense.

What was the value of chastity? Was no sex what Jesus really advocated? Were we not created as sexual beings? I listened to many lectures and discussions describing us humans as basically sexual beings. Really? I thought we humans were basically intelligent beings. Especially those at a university. There were many attractive males on the Notre Dame campus. For the first time, I allowed my body to tingle when I saw a good-looking male. That was an experience I had not had since high school. I was aware I was changing. Why did I have these feelings if they weren't good? It didn't make very much sense to me. I suppose this new, still unattractive habit did not call for sexual attention.

When living in my community, I refrained from asking these questions. Only the one view, the medieval view of the Catholic Church's value of sex, infused my mind. I accepted it without exposure and serious thought. The conversations with my fellow students, with the theological discussions ever present on campus, and encounters with so many intelligent, exceptionally honest people, opened my mind. My male fellow students were my friends, and I became as comfortable with them as I did with my sisters in Lewis Hall. I still believed in my vow of chastity, yet my body was telling me that some of these males were not only intellectually stimulating but magnetically attractive. I was on guard to protect my vow.

Lastly, where did the vow of obedience fit into my life? Was I willing to hand over the submission of my intellectual conclusions, of my will, to other human beings who believed differently? I no longer accepted the infallibility of the Pope. Nor did many of the Church's great theologians. How was I going to believe that my superiors were always right and always pure in their motives? I recalled my Uncle Joe's goodbye message to me before I entered the convent, "You know you will have to do everything they tell you, and you don't like to obey. Are you sure you want to take this step?" I did stop and think about those words, but as an idealist, I marched on as though I could overcome that independent spirit. Uncle Joe knew me better than I knew myself. I liked the freedom that Notre Dame gave me.

On July 25, 1968, the Encyclical called *Humanae Vitae* declared that women had no control over their bodies. This document condemned both birth control, pre-marital sex, and abortion. Pope John XXIII was dead, and his successor, Paul VI, was closing the windows. The air would get stale. By the time Pope Paul VI issued this document, most married women of childbearing age had decided that the Church had no authority in their bedrooms. The Church lost its moral authority on sex through this document.

While the Catholic hierarchy holds firm to this doctrine, birth control is widely practiced by 97% of Catholic women of childbearing age. Catholics ignore the admonition against premarital sex and live together quite publicly without guilt. I had grown in sync with the majority of Catholics on the intellectual issues of sex in the Church. But by the time I graduated at 32, I was still a virgin.

THE PRESSURE GROWS

Among the religious who discovered that life outside the convent did not mean abandoning the Church, I found a new identity during this period of upheaval while a student at Notre Dame. During my life in Lewis Hall, I was surrounded by the brightest minds who were dedicated and committed to the importance of being true to oneself, serving those less fortunate, working for social justice, and centering their lives in the midst of all this new direction. Many of these women were leaving their communities, and my conversations with them encouraged me to rethink my commitment.

The pressure was on for decision-making. I expected to finish my dissertation in the early spring and graduate in May. I had been praying and reflecting for a year on what my future might hold. I surprised myself at how calm I was as I looked to the future. Somehow I knew my life would work out.

Away from my religious community for nearly four years, I had little communication with anyone there during that time. I had to admit that the few friends from the community that I had were those with whom

I went to summer classes at Notre Dame. After 14 years, they were the only two sisters in the community with whom I could confide. That realization in itself was depressing.

When I returned for retreat the summer before my last year in graduate school, I had an experience that only added to my confusion about religious life. I dropped by to visit one of the nuns I knew fairly well who was assigned to the college. I had been told that my Ph.D. would prepare me for an administrative officer position, more than likely Dean and then President. I wanted to get her input about what life at the college would be like.

Since I had not seen her around, I checked her office with no luck. Even checking on her cell door several times, I came up empty. I tried to slip a note under her door, but it was impossible. Finally on the last day of retreat, I checked the door and discovered it unlocked. So I opened the door to drop the note inside. To my amazement, chagrin, and disappointment, I found her and her lover in bed. Acting as though I was invisible, they said not a word to me. I closed the door, walked down the stairs and out into the campus. I found a retreat in the grotto among the trees, and it came to me: "I do not want to be here." Was I disturbed because they were lesbian? Undoubtedly.

I never saw either of these nuns after opening that bedroom door. I never had a conversation with them about their feelings for one another. I never had a conversation about homosexuality with any gay man or lesbian. I was ignorant.

The next day, I left to visit with my parents. I went back to Notre Dame with no answers to my questions about the college and without having any discussions about my future with anyone, including the Mother General or her assistants who made the assignments.

By December following that summer at Marywood, I had had conversations with a few dear friends at Notre Dame about my future. Eventually I made my decision after struggling with my vow. I had promised Jesus. Was I giving up on Him? I had learned through my study and prayer that Jesus wanted all of us to be happy. That included me.

In my deliberation to leave my religious community, I thought the right thing to do was to request a leave of absence for a year. That was what nuns who were planning to leave were doing. It seemed to me that, after 14 years, I should not make a rash decision. I requested that leave of absence in a letter to the Mother General. The response came in an unexpected phone call from one of her assistants. She was cold and curt.

"Why do you want a leave of absence? Why don't you just go? If you know you want to leave, then just ask to be released from your vows."

I assumed she had no empathy for keeping anyone on the books who was thinking about leaving. Normally I would have shaken in my shoes to be talking to her at all. I had a previous encounter with her in my first year when I had to ask for a small amount of money because that poor kid in South Bend had stolen mine and I had not yet received my fellowship. She sent the check with a yellow sticky note, "Use it carefully." I always had this feeling that she did not agree with the decision to send me to graduate school, and now she seemed to be pushing me away from the community as fast as she could.

Something snapped in me. It may have been God giving me a push,but my answer to her was, "Oh, I thought I should take the time. Thank you. I'll write another letter requesting permanent release from my vows." The call probably took no more than five minutes, but it was life-changing. From that moment forward, I knew that my decision was right. Regrets did not find room in my closet, and nothing would stop me from changing my clothes and my life.

Now I really had to worry. How was I going to make a living? With only six months to go before I could work, I still had my fellowship, but the expenses were piling up. I had to pay to have my dissertation professionally typed which in 1970 was $485. My papers from the Vatican arrived in March with a check for $300 from the religious community, the same amount my dowry contributed 14 years earlier. No good wishes accompanied the check. A number of my friends in graduate school had left their communities, and their treatment differed from mine. Their communities were sad to see them go, but good wishes assured them of their prayers and support for their wellbeing.

One of these friends was my career angel. I had applied to several colleges and universities for positions but by April had found very little response. The economy in 1970 was not thriving. Colleges and universities were also struggling. To cut costs and to offer students greater opportunities, work was underway to join together in consortiums and even in mergers. Since I had worked on the unsuccessful St. Mary's - Notre Dame merger and my dissertation was an in-depth study of two confederations of higher education that worked quite well, I was sure I should be able to find a job.

A Franciscan, Miriam, requested to be released from her vows, as did her fiancé, John, a Christian Brother. John was the Academic Dean at the College of St. Francis. St. Francis and Lewis College, a neighboring male institution run by the Christian Brothers, were preparing for a merger with a reorganization of the administration underway. With Miriam's influence, her fiancé recommended me for the position of Associate Provost, and I was hired.

Because the start date was July 1, I had two months to figure out how I would live. The university kept me on for the month of May. My parents, my brother John (a newly ordained priest), and my uncle, Father Leo, drove out to Notre Dame for my graduation. John came to my rescue. Since he received an old car from Father Leo for his ordination the previous year, he was willing to sell it to me for $500, which I could pay him after I got on my feet. His pastor was buying him a new one. My parents had very little money. Retired and living on social security, they could not help.

Although I left the convent, I did not abandon my faith. I continued to pray and trust in Divine Providence. For me, God took on Her feminine nature. Because men were in control over the last thousands of years, they had declared God to be male and all references to God were male. Some of us at Notre Dame decided that this did not have to continue. If we were made in God's image and likeness, then, for us women, She was female. So I did pray to Her, often with great intensity.

I had to look for an apartment to live in Joliet, Illinois, where I would work, but I needed a security deposit and the first month's rent, another $500. Miriam and John came to the rescue again. John got an advance on my salary for me before he left his job. Amazed at the power that he had, I wondered if I would be able to influence lives for the good as he had done.

My fellow graduate students came from myriad backgrounds. Their diversity of interests and experiences inspired me to discover why such good people did not choose religious life. They had the same dedication to service that I had. I mingled with lay students seeking doctorates in both secular and religious fields, with priests from dioceses or religious orders who were also evaluating their lives. By the time I received my doctorate, I had left my religious community, was released from my vows, and faced a new reality: making a living on my own.

I had a lot of growing up and a lot of learning to do. But moving on to my first outside job was a shocking experience. No vow of poverty now to sustain my daily life; no vow of chastity to protect me from falling in lust, to say nothing of love; and no vow of obedience to burden my spirit. This new freedom was frightening.

PART THREE

A Leap into
The World

CHAPTER FOURTEEN

A Female Voice Among Men

Life tumbled at me like raging waters, and I barely knew how to swim in this new ocean of college administration. The St. Francis - Lewis merger had been in process for two years, and everyone seemed to be worn down by the lack of progress when I arrived in Joliet to lend my so-called "merger expertise." For the woman who saw herself as a guppy in this new ocean of life, the title of Associate Provost seemed pretentious.

As we prepared for the first step of a merger, allowing students to take classes from either college for the upcoming fall season, discussions often broke down over schedules and finances. Both colleges feared losing control to the other. Each had its own gender culture which boards, administration, faculty, staff, and alumni strove to protect. Beneath the clouds of fear on both sides, power and status were always present, especially with the male institution. The Christian Brothers' attitude and that of the Lewis faculty bordered on misogyny. The atmosphere sent me scurrying to find support among the women faculty and staff.

The tension and hostility about the merger targeted those of us who were new as enemies in the battle if we were not always on alert. I had academic experience with the proposed merger between Notre Dame and St. Mary's College. But I did not have much experience with the personal affronts that go with the games people play to assume power. Initially, Frank Kerins, the President of St. Francis, saw to my education about this. He discussed the steps that needed to be taken to succeed with certain personalities and to ignore others. With Frank's help, these guys were not going to get me. I found the new me. I worked and I studied, persuading some on occasion but not others.

In the midst of this, I waited for each payday to settle in at my apartment. I barely could afford food much less a bed, living room furniture, or a kitchen table. Each Saturday morning, I would search the garage sale ads in the paper, grab my pitiable purse, and head for the neighborhoods for a lamp here, a chair there, some pots and pans, and a few dishes. I needed a mattress, and I wanted it to be new, so I learned about credit for this first important purchase.

The few clothes I had were not going to make it. I had accumulated a few outfits during the last six months at Notre Dame — not a nun habit but definitely not professional or stylish. A white blouse and a navy-blue skirt would not cut it. The green-and-navy plaid blazer added some style, but the outfit just shouted former nun.

My new women acquaintances introduced me to consignment shops and JC Penney. I also needed something done with my hair, and since JC Penney provided clothes, why not take advantage of their beauty salon? I had no advice on this decision. The styles at the time demanded that I get some curl in my hair. Long, dark, very fine hair did not take well to the Penney's permanent. I looked like Godzilla and smelled like ammonia. I couldn't afford another treatment or a cut. For months, the hair was pulled back off my face in a ponytail.

All of the leaders involved in the merger, other than me, were men. I graduated from Marywood, our small IHM Catholic women's college, and I supported the value it contributed to women's education. It gave women the opportunity to develop their talents and skills without the interference of the battle of the sexes. One of my tasks professionally, as well as one I valued personally, was to assure that the strengths of this woman's college were not weakened. But I had to make my points behind closed doors with Frank Kerins. I did not attend the negotiations. The teams had no tolerance for a woman, even an observer. I did not press the issue.

The atmosphere lacked trust, not only because of the serious financial threats, but also because it seemed everyone lacked an appreciation of the other's strengths. This distrust, along with the amount of hostility that existed between the leaders of each college and their respective staffs, was not a good omen. From the very beginning, I suspected they lacked the will to determine what was best for the future of each school. Power struggles produce this lack of will. The merger failed.

Both colleges were left to overcome their own financial difficulties. St. Francis chose a slower, more determined plan to success. Lewis College went big. It became a university and hired its first lay president and four new deans. I left St. Francis and I became the Dean of the College of Continuing Education, an exciting and challenging task.

START A COLLEGE?

This was only my second year out of graduate school, and I was selected to get a new college off the ground. I figured I would have plenty of help since Lewis already offered evening classes to working adults. I had no idea how difficult it was to gather agreement from those who have plenty of skin in the game. My mission was to develop degree programs for working adults who had a variety of backgrounds, bring in new students. When we announced that we would evaluate backgrounds and give credit for previous study and work achievements, the applications flooded in. I was dependent on the Faculty of Liberal Arts and the College of Business to support the program. And that presented a major problem.

The Dean of Business and his faculty strongly disagreed with the concept of a separate college for adults and giving college credit for experience. His previous success was based on building their student population with evening classes for working adults. He feared his numbers would decrease, and he fought it with all his weapons. Sometimes he scared me — a foot taller than me and with a commanding voice of righteous academia, he came into my office. No "good morning." No "hi, how are you?" Just,

"I took a vote of the faculty and they do not approve of giving credit for work. We are a quality academic institution, and we will only give credit for class attendance and work. You have very

little experience in college administration. Maybe the College of St. Francis will compromise their reputation, but we will not.

I'm afraid it's out of our hands, my friend. The Board of Trustees and the President have already given permission to review people's experience. Students will be interviewed, and we will determine together in each situation what is credit-worthy. In some cases, it may require an essay or a thesis. We hope your faculty will determine this for the business students and advise us.

Lady, as long as I'm Dean, this will not happen".

And he left. I wanted to say, "Dr. Jordan to you," but I held my tongue. The dean had pretty strong tools to prove his point. He was male, in a doctoral program in business at Illinois Technology, had considerable experience as a faculty member and a department head, and was well respected by his peers and his students. I, female with a Notre Dame doctorate and knowledge of mergers, had very little experience as a faculty member or a college administrator. I had almost no support from faculty or department heads, and I was implementing the policies of the barely known president. The battle was on.

The Board of Trustees were counting on the College of Continuing Education to bring in hundreds of new students and to develop a new image to market to its donors. Going big was a real risk. The College of Continuing Education had everything to lose. Luckily, we had the authority of the president with the backing of the Board of Trustees.

In the convent, the power struggles were very limited. One always accepted God's will, which was the will of the superior, whoever she may be. We were her children. She spoke, we obeyed. It was not so in the college atmosphere. Leaders saw faculty as prima donnas. Faculty saw administrators as imposing on their freedom to teach. I knew this through my studies, but I didn't fully grasp how broad and intense the turf battles could become.

A College of Continuing Education was a relatively new concept in 1971, with very few models to draw upon. At Lewis, we would not compromise quality, but we had to fight the faculty's unreasonable determination of quality. They objected to giving college credit for previous work accomplished in a field of study, a practice well-known today but very new in 1972.

The president was supportive and dedicated to getting continuing education off and running. We meshed well in the incipient stages, plus his backing gave me some power with the faculty and department heads. When the Dean of Business saw that our first semester of classes had doubled the enrollment of his evening classes, with the accompanying finances, he stopped fighting us.

INITIATING PRISONER EDUCATION

Beginning on-site college classes at Statesville Penitentiary, a maximum-security prison, was the brainchild of the president. These classes produced the first campus prison program in the State of Illinois and the first prisoner to earn a bachelor's degree not only in the State of Illinois but perhaps in the country. That prisoner, William Heirens, had been a brilliant 15-year-old freshman at the University of Chicago when he was convicted for the murder of a seven-year-old girl that made national headlines in the fifties. His story appears in many college sociology books discussing whether he was tried by the press. I got to know Heirens fairly well, and like nearly all prisoners, he claimed his innocence. Would DNA have proved his innocence? Over the then 20-some years of his imprisonment, the staff were never convinced either way.

Perhaps it was William Heiren's 180 IQ that provoked the doubts. He had completed many correspondence courses from universities across the nation. He had more than enough credits to meet Lewis University's criteria for graduation. All he needed was to complete his final 12 hours with us, and that he did in one semester with our faculty at the prison. Our College of Continuing Education landed on the pages of many newspapers across the country with a photo of my conferring his degree. My mother didn't want to announce in her local paper that

I got my doctorate in 1970 from the University of Notre Dame, lest she be embarrassed at my having left the convent. Now she saw me in cap and gown with a well-known prisoner on the front pages of the national newspapers.

The opposition to awarding credit for experience paled in comparison to that of enrolling prisoners on campus. The prisoners who were allowed to enroll were in a halfway program that got them ready for parole. The selection was done by a committee of male prison administrators. The first day a prisoner in civilian clothes walked across campus, he stopped a female student and announced, "If you knew that I just came from prison, I bet you'd be running away from me,"

And run, she did. Luckily, she was mature enough to report it to her professor, and I got a call before the class started: "Do we have prisoners on campus?"

Of course I had to tell him the truth, "Yes, is there a problem?"

The president wrongly wanted the prisoners to simply fit in with the students and not alert the faculty or students to the prisoners' presence. I thought the faculty should know who they had in class. The president's decision certainly backfired. I immediately contacted the director of the halfway house, and he was on campus within five minutes, rescuing us by removing that prisoner. They had no women on their prisoner screening team and no women in their prison classes. This prisoner had not seen a beautiful, young 20-year-old in ten years. He did not know how to react, and he wanted her attention. He thought he'd be "cute."

We also initiated a degree program in social justice for police. That program drew enormous numbers from the Cook County Sheriff's Office and the City of Chicago. By the end of my second year, we had increased the student enrollment at Lewis by over a thousand students. Imagine police and prisoners on a free and open campus together. It worked after we all became better educated about the prisoner selection process.

Getting these continuing education programs off the ground was exhilarating. The proof of their growth indicated that this concept was needed and workable. Yet the ever-present tension between the faculty and administration as well as the undertow of rip tides within the administration got to me. During my third year, I began searching for a new position.

At one of our weekly deans' meetings in the president's office, we were all struck by the sound of a tape recorder reaching its end. The president jumped up, yelled, "that's a fire alarm," and sent us out of his office. No one else was moving in the building, and the top university administrators looked like idiots milling around outside his office while he was evidently changing the tape. When we returned to the meeting, this ruse was easily foiled when the Dean of Nursing, at least 30 years my senior with white hair and unequivocal confidence and audacity, spoke out. "Sounded like a tape recorder to me. Were you taping us, sir?"

"Of course not. I've no idea what that alarm was," he tried to explain. We didn't know how often and for how long he had been taping us or what he would use these tapes for. This of course tore down whatever walls of trust were built with the president, each of us struggling with our own suspicions about his intentions on any subject.

A rather good-looking, very sexy young Italian man came on as Director of Development. Eight years younger than I, vibrant, and ready to help this University, he was just right for this fundraising job. He was only 25, but I loved the excitement we both had when we were together. We began to support one another when the usual tensions of college administration got to us. I liked his admiration and respect for me, and his sensuality. Whenever he saw me, his smile would broaden and his eyes would light up. And I got all those tingly feelings telling me ah, the chemistry was there.

We began to date. No policy existed that forbade it, but we did try to be careful on campus. We kept it professional when we were working, but it was exciting to be with him after hours. I had dated several men from the college, but this was my first boyfriend.

He became concerned about my safety after I had several threatening phone calls. The voice on the phone was muffled. I suspected it was someone at the college who was screaming some pretty filthy words and threatening to kill me. Since we had policemen from Chicago available, I asked their advice. They, too, were concerned about my safety. One brought me some pepper spray, and another advised that I get a dog who could alert me to danger if someone did break in.

The hours at Lewis were very long. Continuing Education offered classes well into the evening, and I often had to be there. Because I felt it wouldn't be fair to leave the dog in the apartment all day, my boyfriend offered to keep it at his house on campus during the day. His suggestion was that I should get a toy Manchester Terrier to protect me. Since I lived in an apartment, the dog had to be small. This breed of brown-and-black toy terriers was protective, known for its alertness and feistiness. I agreed, and I found a breeder with a six-month old, very well trained Manchester Terrier, whom I named Sasha.

Sasha proved to be all I expected. One night when I opened the door to my apartment, this little eight-pound security dog stopped at the door. He began to follow a trail with his nose. My body shook with fright. Was someone there? I couldn't move from the doorway. Sasha finally returned and sat at my feet. It was safe. The next day, the apartment manager told me that the repair man was in my apartment to fix a window. No doubt, Sasha smelled his presence.

My boyfriend loved cars, and I loved riding in his 1973 Corvette or his 1972 Buick Riviera. One day when he was driving my 1963 Plymouth to work in seven inches of snow, after he had spent the night at my house, we crashed into another sliding vehicle. Both of us survived with minor injuries, but the car did not. No longer were we able to keep our relationship private at the university. We were late arriving at work, and it was hard to come up with an excuse of why we were bandaged up. We had spent most of the day in the hospital. We had to call his twin sister to come and get us and drive us to his home on campus. For me, the ex-nun, it was embarrassing. For him, not so much.

Our relationship lasted two years. During that time, he came home to meet my parents at Christmas, and I had spent many Sundays at his parents' home for a multi-course Italian dinner. Even at 13 years of age when I first became interested in boys, it was the Italian ones that turned me on, much to my parents' chagrin. Why couldn't I just like the Irish boys? It appeared that Italian parents didn't like the Irish any more than my parents liked the Italians. It was clear his parents didn't like our age difference either. Would I want children at my age? I had not made that decision yet.

As relationships sometimes go, the fire was dying, but the final break was my decision to leave Lewis University.

CHAPTER FIFTEEN

A Different World

FOR THE FIRST TIME IN MY LIFE, at the age of 36, I stepped out of the daily world of the Catholic Church. I accepted a job with General Motors Institute (GMI) at their Management Education Department in Flint, Michigan. Most jobs are attained through connections, and this was no exception. My dear friend's dear friend talked to her dear friend, the CEO of GM. The timing was right since the GMI executives were looking for minorities and women to meet their affirmative action plan. This was July 1973, and the women's movement was in its prime as I walked into a universe that would change my life.

Three very powerful women on the staff of GMI recognized their place in time to transform the attitude of General Motors management: Helen Moye, Char McCrae, and Karen Silver. These women raised me from the kindergarten program I began in feminism at Notre Dame to feminism on the grand scale of activism that prepared me for my future. Each of us taught an average of 25 managers every week, and we had the opportunity to lead them in their thinking about women. A small number of union women from the GM plants and headquarters dusted each class with some feminism, but most had bought the line that they had to be like men to succeed, because in the beginning, we did. I recognized that contradiction because I, too, had believed it.

INITIATING CHANGE

Most of those managers, with few exceptions, were overwhelmed by the concept of equality for women. In an atmosphere of cultural change, it is very difficult when your bosses are blind to the need for change. But when you have one or two managers who support your efforts, as we did, it became possible to achieve change.

The change we were after was three-fold:

1. to convince our bosses of the inequality that existed for women and what we could do as management trainers to erase the injustice from our system;

2. to convince the managers in the field who supervised women not only of the barriers in the system that existed for women to succeed, but also of the action they needed to take; and

3. to convince the women of their role in helping all of us to change the system that existed.

These were indeed mammoth challenges. These three women, Moye, McCrae, and Silver, had been working on three training programs for at least a year by the time I arrived at GMI. They did the research by studying what was in print, interviewing women in GM headquarters to get information and support. They kept this project under lock and key until they were sure they would be successful. We four women jumped in to convince our bosses of the necessity for three new training programs to effect these changes to assimilate women into the company.

At first we were more successful in convincing the women to gain achievements for themselves in the company. The women learned the value of becoming assertive and of speaking out for what they wanted. The managers were not so sure. They became threatened when women wanted to get promoted, and the men complained. Change had begun and we were encouraged.

It was clear that our managers did not consider these three new programs as valuable as the other management classes. Their concern, they said, was that our reputations would be hurt if we let these women and minority programs take priority. Our managers said they "did not want us saddled with the 'women's program'" lest we be tainted and not accepted as capable to train all levels. As much passion as we had for these programs, we understood that our bosses were right. This was not a GM priority in its dominantly male environment.

General Motors offered me many other opportunities to grow in those first months. I had several fellow male professionals who guided my way. Since the actual content for the management courses was very familiar to me, a fellow project manager, Roger Montgomery, requested that I shadow him when he went to the factories. I was unfamiliar with how the manufacturing operations worked. I did not understand the daily tasks of the supervisors and managers whom I interacted with in the classroom.

Roger arranged for me to observe assembly line after assembly line in Buick, Oldsmobile, Pontiac, Cadillac, and Chevrolet; and he accompanied me. I traveled to plants that forged the steel, built batteries, constructed the differentials, and even to the research centers where new products were being designed. Roger became my mentor and led me to any success I had at GM.

Barry Roach, out of the office in Rochester, New York, invited me to join a team to study systems management for the corporation. This team, composed of people with exceptional backgrounds with at least master's degrees, met one weekend a month in Buffalo, New York, to create a program that would train executives in systems management. Coincidentally or subconsciously planned, all six members of the team had previously been a member of a religious ministry: two ex-priests, one Lutheran minister, two ex-nuns, and a Mormon Bishop. We all had graduate studies in systems theory, but what did a religious orientation have to do with those studies, if anything? Perhaps we were chosen because we all broke away from rigid institutions and wanted to create the openness of new systems not only into our own lives but into the corporate life of GM. The project stimulated my creative juices, and I looked forward to this post-graduate experience each month with great anticipation.

THE UNIVERSITY OF MICHIGAN

Many of the project managers and supervisors at GMI also taught as lecturers in the University of Michigan's Management Education Division of the School of Business. Helen Moye and a few of the others often asked me to team teach with one of them or to take one of their classes as a substitute. This opportunity would never have come if I had not been at General Motors, and it contributed to the groundwork for my future entrepreneurial efforts.

On April 15, 1974, after only nine months on the job, supercharged with these new experiences of women's programs, executive seminars, the systems theory team, teaching at the University of Michigan, the fan blew the detritus, and I got hit badly. My supervisor called me into his office and announced that GMI had to lay off ten people, and because the last one hired was number one to be let go, my name occupied first place on the list. A serious energy crisis had hit America, and GM experienced it for the first time in its 75-year history. The ten of us marked for dismissal happened to be women and minorities who were the last hired: PhDs, attorneys, business people, and graduate students who left good jobs 10 to 15 months earlier.

We thought it didn't make much sense for GM to dismantle the greatest part of its progress with affirmative action. But affirmative action went out the GM window. The corporation relied on its old policy that was set up with both the union and management, "Last In, First Out (LIFO)."

For anyone at GM less than a year, one received two weeks' notice with an additional two weeks of severance pay, not enough to pay my rent and feed myself before I found a job. If I had been there a full year, as the other nine were, I would have had a much more substantial benefit package. I had spent all of my savings on my move the previous July. Unemployment would not kick in for at least a month. My first instinct was to fight back.

With affirmative action in mind, I contacted a female lawyer who informed me, "No one sues GM and wins, especially with the judges here in Michigan. Give it up." I appealed to the higher levels within GMI but they, worrying about their own jobs, reached for their swords: "What makes you think you're exceptional? What makes you think you're that good?" posed the managing director.

Wow! The answer that buzzed in my head to the questions: "Because you told me so; you put it in writing, dummy." But no, I didn't say that. I knew better as I sat at one end of a very long conference table and he and his two sidekicks, one my manager, sat at the other.

My real response was that I received the highest evaluations both from the students and my superiors, the marvelous student response, and the work that had been accomplished. All to no avail. Feeling the loss of that battle, I reached down for the courage to do what I should have done in the beginning, look for a new job.

My co-workers at GMI were fantastic. Jerry Reid and Helen Moye offered to let me have their outside assignments at the University of Michigan Management School so that I could make some money. Barry Roach, my supportive systems manager who had seen the writing on the wall, had left the previous month for a new position at Martin Marietta. He called to offer me an interview with his new boss for a position as Manager of the Management Education Department. I begged off, not sure that I wanted to go to Florida.

CHAPTER SIXTEEN

Creating a Plan

Helen Moye and I had become close friends. Married and divorced twice with three children to raise as a single mother, she developed a plan to apply her business goal-setting skills to her personal life. She had set out a plan to get married, but this time she wanted to marry someone who would be her mate for life.

At 5' 3" and 150 pounds with a deep brown, silky complexion and eyes that sparkled when she laughed, she had set her criteria for the kind of man she wanted to marry. Having had plenty of experience of the kind she did not want to marry, her success within six months was amazing. She had met a fellow on an airplane, Sam, to whom she became engaged. But when a friend introduced Helen to Henry Moye, she traded Sam's engagement ring for Henry's love. Six months later she was married to Henry. They remained married 36 years until her death in 2009.

Of course, in Helen's mind, there was no reason why I couldn't meet my life partner as she did. One Sunday afternoon in early January she invited me to her house, having sent her daughters, 16-year-old Simone and her pre-teen Opella, out with Henry for the afternoon. With the steady assurance of a woman who knew how she got married, she placed a crystal glass half-full of Johnny Walker Red in my right hand and a pen and tablet in my left. Together we drew up my plan. Yes, I actually drew up this plan to get married. Was I just nuts?

Objective: To be married in a year.

Goal: To set criteria for the man you want to marry.

Activity: Get Looking.

First step: Send out the message tomorrow, "I want to get married."

We spent some time drawing up the criteria for what I thought would be important for me. He doesn't have to be wealthy, but he has to have a job. I'm not going to be the sole support. I would like him to be around my age. Let's say between 35-50. Most of all, he has to be interesting, have his own interests. I want him to be willing to communicate and to be honest. Trustworthy, of course. And he can't be divorced or have kids.

With those deep brown eyes, staring directly in my face and questioning my sanity, Helen was incredulous.

"That just doesn't make any sense. If you look at the age you selected and that he can't be divorced and have children, you have severely limited the available population. I would say, throw away this goal. The chances that you are going to meet someone is very close to zero."

She paused and then added, "Why can't he be divorced?"

In my head the answer was, *Catholic girls do not marry divorced men.* Of course, my family's reaction to my marrying a divorced man was hovering over me as I remained silent.

"You are going to have a very difficult time finding a man with these other criteria who has not been married with children." I knew that Helen was making sense, but the stereotype of a man with children sat firmly in my head. I felt I would be asking for problems. If he had kids and couldn't stay married, why could I trust him? Frightened enough about marriage, I couldn't fathom having children. How would I accept raising someone else's? The no divorce, no children criteria stood firm.

One of Helen's steps in the plan was no sex before commitment. Helen had been married twice and had plenty of sex partners, but this was different. She convinced me that women looked at sex differently at that time. "Once the fellow had sex," she opined, "if that's all he wants in the relationship, he will either continue to date you on that condition or drop you." Did I object to casual sex? Not really, although Helen seemed to be more comfortable with the concept than I. Her point in refusing sex until a commitment was made enforced the seriousness one required in the relationship. I bought into that.

Although Helen's plan worked for her, I had lingering doubts of letting such an approach work for me. A great deal of faith was necessary for this goal-setting to work. Once I made up my mind that this is what I wanted in life, I knew I had to commit to the plan each day.

One of the most important elements of Helen's plan and one of the most difficult was to share the goal with someone who could help you. Indicating to Helen that I would sound desperate if I shared this goal with others, she responded,

"If you were desperate, you would have taken any man. You didn't and you won't. Why shouldn't you be in control of getting married? Why should we, supposedly sophisticated women, wait until the 'right man' comes around and decides he is the one for us? You set goals to get your degree. You even set goals to go to Europe. You planned, you sacrificed other things while you saved your money. Why wouldn't you have a plan for the most important decision in your life, finding a man who would be your life mate?"

If I were to follow her advice and her example, I had to dig deeply for the courage to announce, "I want to get married before my birthday, 11 months from now, December 7, 1974." If you have never done anything like this where you put yourself out there against the world which could shout "that's stupid" or "you'll look desperate," then you might not know what courage it takes. It is friggin' scary. But Helen insisted it was necessary and that I should start on Monday morning when I went to work. If I didn't tell someone my plan the very next day, then when would I?

I decided that the best and first one to tell would be my friend and colleague, Roger Montgomery, who had voluminous connections out in the field and could introduce me to some eligible prospects. On Monday morning, with nerves twittering and stomach turning, I asked Roger to the cafeteria for coffee and announced, "Roger, I want to get married." His response, "Wait a few months, I'll divorce Barbara and marry you."

He did not take me seriously, and this angered me. No longer was this Helen's goal but mine. Why couldn't I find someone and get married in a year? All kinds of people get married, every race, every creed, big hulks, small dainty ones, educated and uneducated ones, and all these sometimes marry each other. By the end of the day, the word was out at GMI, and I had plenty of offers to help me.

By April, I had no serious relationship when GM laid me off. I had to find a job, so I felt I had to change my goal. Helen was not buying such reasoning. She insisted this may be God's way to get me to the place where I would meet "him."

Barry Roach, my former colleague on the Systems Management Team at General Motors, had tried several times to convince me to come to Florida for the interview.

Finally, I told him, "Barry, I really want to get married. Actually, I set a goal to get married by my birthday in December."

"Did you meet someone?"

"Uh, no. But starting off in a new place, I think the odds are against me."

Just like Helen, Barry would have none of that excuse. He and his boss, Winter, the Vice President of Human Resources, were determined to get a program in management education underway.

"Aggie, you can find somebody here as well as in Michigan. We probably have plenty of bachelors here at Martin Marietta." Barry evidently thought this plan was easy. Set the objective and do it. I did not see it that way.

"Barry, I do have some criteria. I'm not just going to marry anyone."

Since Barry didn't get anywhere with that call, a week later he phoned me with some data that he gathered.

"Aggie, I got the personnel people to look up some information. We have 2,000 single men here at Martin between the ages of 35-50. I will help you find someone. I've talked to my boss, Winter. He says he will help you. He knows lots of single people."

If Barry and his boss were willing to hire me and not think of me as just plain nuts, then I'm going to take the job. After some serious churning about another move within a year, leaving Michigan, Helen, and my other friends, I accepted the job at Martin Marietta. On July 1, I started as Manager of Management Education.

CHAPTER SEVENTEEN

Working the Plan

IFOUND THE ADJUSTMENT TO MARTIN MARIETTA very difficult. The positive atmosphere at GMI had spoiled me. Except for that last meeting with the three managers, I never experienced any feeling of deliberate insult, or behavior, or treatment that was not respectful. Competition, yes. Meanness, no.

The military atmosphere of an aerospace company usually developed because of its practice of recruiting managers from the military. After the generals and colonels, majors, and captains (almost all men in 1974) had retired or resigned from the military, they often took a job in the defense industry. Even formerly enlisted men who spent much time in the service were part of the recruitment field for defense contractors. We non-military personnel in human resources recognized how deeply we would have to delve to reorganize these manager's attitudes. Barry had little trouble teaching the managers, but I became the symbol for change and a target for their anger. The men accepted that women had their place as secretaries, but for those women who wanted to progress into supervisory positions on the line or in procurement, it was a battle that the executives had to be willing to take on. Were they capable of change?

This military atmosphere controlled any change the company tried to make with managers. This included moving women into management. One manager proclaimed out loud in a class I was holding, "You don't understand, Lady, women just won't be able to handle these managers. They will be crying at the first insult. You couldn't do it."

Well, here was my insult, how would I react? My response had to prove the opposite of this manager's belief.

"I'm sure there are strong women here at Martin who would qualify for the supervisory level. I've talked to some that can't wait to get promoted to supervisor. They didn't act like they would be very intimidated. Women are certainly qualified at General Motors. Why do you think the women that Martin hires would be less qualified?"

"I know women and they just can't cut it."

"Do any of you know a woman who could be promoted to supervisor?" I asked.

The hands flew up. "My secretary could do it." Another, "My wife could do it — but she doesn't work here. She manages me." Everyone laughed. The managers carried the discussion. That insult opened up the possibilities.

As difficult as it was for women, it was even more difficult for black men and women to assimilate into the company. One of my first tasks was to hire an African American consultant to help us establish a program for integrating minorities into this rigid atmosphere of prejudice. As Barry and I struggled with this program, we finally decided that we should try to get Helen to help us. Helen was still full-time at General Motors Institute, but she was able to take some time off to consult with us. She helped us develop a program to sensitize managers to the need for including minorities and women in the workplace. Our plan was for Helen and me to offer the pilot program, then after we had brought it to where we believed it was successful, we would hire trainers to run it.

Helen had a very engaging personality and had great success at GMI and the University of Michigan with similar programs, but she met much resistance and even some verbal abuse in this seminar at Martin Marietta. Embarrassed and angry that the managers would treat Helen with such intolerance, I learned that their southern politeness was a myth when it came to race and gender discussions. We were stunned by the attacks of racist and misogynist language directed at us in the classroom.

"Women and black people are not ready to join an aerospace corporation,"

"We draw our people from the military."

"Blacks are not educated and I'm not sure they can be."

"You girls may be okay, but most girls can't do this work."

It went on from there. These were the managers of the departments; what would it be like when we started to train their subordinates?

At the end of the week of training, our heads were pounding and our spirits quite deflated. Helen stayed for the weekend to relax, but she decided she did not want to tackle these managers in Orlando again.

I had little choice. The program, as it was, was not working. We had experienced similar reactions at GM but not as hostile an audience, nor with managers attending the University of Michigan workshops. Usually with our program structure we witnessed the breakdown of the resistance at the end of the first day of class. Then learning would take hold on the second day.

Barry, Winter, and I decided that these managers were not ready for these programs. We had to dig deeper and start all over again. There evidently had to be a system change before we could subject any trainers to that abuse. We would have to start from the top with the executives. And Winter would start working behind the scenes with the executive committee. We turned our attention to other programs until the time was ripe for us to begin again.

This experience with the efforts to assimilate women and minorities tainted my other feelings about working at Martin. My social life was nearly barren. Barry and Winter did keep their word about introducing me to eligible men. But after a few efforts, I told them they didn't have to do the work, I would. Through their introductions, I sat across a few dinner tables with some boring guys, at least boring to me.

One morning, dropping my change into the coffee machine, Ed, an acquaintance whose desk was near the vending machines, called to me as he stood next to a good-looking man. "Angie (he could never remember my name), come here. I want you to meet a buddy of mine, Robert DeLaurenti. He works in procurement upstairs."

Being introduced to this handsome, fit, male specimen with shining blue eyes and a magnetic smile, I found this gorgeous creature animated, opinionated, and just beautiful. Oh yeah, my body was definitely feeling the vibe. Breathless, I checked out his left hand and spied a college graduation ring in place of a wedding ring. He looked within the age range, and he certainly had a job. My hope rose. All this in 30 seconds at a coffee vending machine. What else? He was Italian.

August 9, 1974, is the marking of another extraordinary historical event. And the vending machine area was buzzing with political chatter. President Richard Nixon had resigned. The Watergate affair had exploded, and now what would happen? Everyone had his (and very few "her") own ideas. Robert, Ed, and I continued our conversation for a few minutes. I returned to my office and started to pray, at the same time wondering, how do I get to meet this guy again?

I didn't have to wait long. At one o'clock, the phone at my desk rang. "Aggie, I'm Robert DeLaurenti. I met you this morning with Ed. I understand you are new here, and I'd love to take you to dinner and get to know you better." When was I available, he asked? Heaven was on the other end of that phone line, and my body and mind were all jitters.

Calm down, girl. Don't sound too anxious. He preempted my response with, "I have Army Reserves on Thursday, but I could make Wednesday evening or tomorrow if you can." *Is two days sufficient to show restraint, I asked myself?*

"Wednesday would be fine," I said as calmly as I could muster. My plan was in action. I began to strengthen my faith in Divine Providence and Helen's goal-setting. And I had not yet been on a single date with this man! We made arrangements for him to pick me up at my apartment on Wednesday evening.

Excited, tripping all over myself, I headed to Barry's office not only to tell him about the date but also to see what he knew about this person. No, he didn't know him, but we did have access to his personnel records. After all, we were in human resources. Looking out for my best interests, Barry captured one of our colleagues, Carol, to bring up Robert's record.

Alarmed, Barry turns to me with his concerned, deep brown Irish eyes, "Aggie, he's married with four kids. You can't go out with him," he said, shaking his black, curly, slightly graying hair as he spouted those damming words.

"What, what are you talking about?" I looked at the record. My heart fell. A woman who wouldn't even date a divorced man just accepted a date with a married man." Miserable, I shouldn't have let this body get so excited.

"Wait a minute," reasonable Carol said. "The man asked you out to dinner. He didn't ask you to marry him. Why don't you keep the date, go out to dinner, and find out if he is still married? If he is, tell him you don't date married men. If he isn't, take it from there."

At that moment, I loved Carol. That made sense. The date was only to check him out anyway.

The evening came for our date. When Robert rang the doorbell, I prayed one last time the mantra ringing in my mind all day — *Oh God, please don't let him be married.* If he were not married but divorced-with-children, how would I feel? At that moment when I opened the door and let him in, my heart jolted. God, he was so good-looking! Dressed in a mauve print shirt with khakis, I hardly noticed he was late, though he was full of apologies.

Within minutes, I learned that the personnel records were outdated by two years. He explained that he had to be sure that his girls, 13 and 16, had their dinner and had settled in for the evening. Within minutes after we started our drive, he told me about his divorce of two years ago and that the other two children, Robbie, 11 years old, and Michelle, barely 7, lived in Seattle with his ex-wife. This man had no secrets. He was quite honest, one of the criteria I valued highly for my life mate. Barry would also be happy to hear this.

We went to dinner at this home-like restaurant on the lake. The owners had turned the residence into a romantic experience for diners. The white tablecloths and burgundy napkins in candlelight set the atmosphere. A band played soft music, and we could hear the water softly lapping against the rocks as we dined. I learned all about his life, and he mine. As an Italian Catholic, he was amazed he had asked out a former nun. After dinner, we went dancing. I felt so right in his arms as we flowed to the music. He was a wonderful dancer, and I felt like Eliza as she sang in *My Fair Lady*:

> *I could have danced all night, I could have danced all night,*
> *And still have begged for more.*
> *I could have spread my wings,*
> *And done a thousand things I've never done before.*
> *I'll never know what made it so exciting.*
> *I only know my heart took flight.*

I did not want this night to end. As we drove home, we didn't stop talking about the dinner, the music, our families. I couldn't ask him in when I arrived at the apartment because my brother and his family were there visiting. So we sat on the interior narrow staircase and continued talking. At this point in the evening, my body and his were pushing me to break my rule of no sex until commitment, means no intercourse until you are both sure you are working toward marriage. But a good night kiss brought the evening to a close.

There was, however, a problem. Robert told me that his ex-wife was arriving at the end of the week. They were going to see if they could put their marriage back together. It had been two years since their divorce, and for the sake of the children, he had agreed to try again. Although devastated, I withheld my feelings from him. He asked me out again for Friday, the night before "she" was to arrive. Torn between messing up what might be a better situation for his family and my own pleasure, I chose another glorious evening.

Barry and Carol were very interested in how the evening had gone. Was he or was he not married? Given the answer, they were now on a mission to update their records. A new project began. Barry, an ex-priest, had no trouble with Robert being divorced. Why would I? Everyone got caught up in my new relationship. Was I in love or was it lust? I did not share with them that Robert's ex-wife was coming down to visit.

The weekend passed very slowly even though my friend Helena, one of my two IHM friends, was visiting and trying to keep me calm. On Monday morning, Robert called and asked me if I could go to lunch with him so that we could talk. He had some work to do, even though he was supposed to be on vacation. Since I didn't know whether the encounter was going to be the end of a very short relationship, anxiety, insecurity, and nervous jitters owned my body. I should have had better control over my emotions. Will this short relationship soon be over? It didn't make much sense to me that Robert had decided about his former marriage in such a few days. But what did I know about him?

When we met, Robert's words filled my heart with joy. Would I just give him a chance to get to know me better? Getting back with his wife was not an option. His marriage had been over, and there was no going back. He said, "I never should have agreed to her coming down."

CHAPTER EIGHTEEN

But He's Divorced with Kids!

I WANTED TO SET ASIDE THE NO DIVORCE, no children criteria, but they kept nagging at me. Robert had called me several times during that week whenever he could get time away and asked for us to spend Saturday evening together after his ex-wife had left for Seattle. I explained that my brother Joe and his family, along with my friend Helena and I, were all planning to go to dinner at Rosie O'Grady's that night. Would he like to join us? Yes, he was delighted to come with us. Rosie's was a fun place with lots of music, and we all enjoyed the evening. When we all arrived home, Robert and I sat on the steps again until 2 a.m. mostly just talking, but with a little kissing. Oh, maybe a little more.

I really wanted to get to know this man. Attraction, lust, perhaps love, and certainly the heart were battling my guilty conscience. If I continued to date this man, then I had to accept that he was divorced-with-children and so far, he was my candidate for marriage. The heart was opening wider. For our third date, Robert asked me to go to the beach in New Smyrna, adding that he would take his daughter, Gina, with us. Gina had been begging to go to the beach. Mary, his older daughter, was working on that Saturday, so she was unable to come.

I was not quite sure that it was a good idea to "meet the kids" so soon, but Robert apparently had no doubts. This would be a good experience for me. The beach was less than an hour away, and Gina entertained me non-stop with a detailed description of the film, *Jeremiah Johnson*. I had not seen the movie but was amazed at her recall of scene after scene of the adventures of Robert Redford's character. I simply listened.

Not only did I learn on this trip that Gina was bright and loquacious, and perhaps a little nervous with me in the passenger seat, but I also saw that she and her dad loved to swim. They did not hesitate to attack the water, running headlong with delight into the waves. Taking the water slowly was my game as I waded with my feet feeling the sand. "Come on out here," Gina urged, and I eventually joined them. As I watched this father-daughter pair teasing each other with how long they could spend underwater, or who could reach the buoy first, I knew this was a family who knew how to have fun. I wanted to be a part of it. So, what about the criteria of a divorced man with kids? It eventually disappeared.

Both Mary and Gina came to Sunday brunch with us. I found the girls intelligent, respectful, and entertaining. Although they loved their mom in Seattle, they also loved their dad and wanted him to be happy. They seemed to be excited about his dating me.

Of course, I called Helen Moye as soon as I knew Robert was a possibility. She could hear in my voice that this man had hooked me.

"Have you told him about your goal?" she questioned. "I can hear in your excitement that you're are falling in love. You're going to get hurt if he doesn't want to get married. You have to tell him without wasting one more day."

I cringed at this step. How do I do this? We had only been on three dates. Wasn't this a little early to be suggesting marriage? Helen's answer came through the telephone receiver, "No, you must tell him so you don't waste time. It's now August. Your goal is December. You don't have much time."

Wow! She brought me back to my goal! Did I just want to have a relationship with a man, or did I want to get married? I definitely wanted to have a relationship *and* I wanted to get married. Robert had all the other important values I set as criteria. In addition to his job, he had taken the responsibility to care for the two oldest children who chose to live with him. He did not back away from any of my inquiries about his marriage and divorce. He was a Major in the Army Reserves and kept his weekly commitment as well as his two weeks away at summer camp. At 39 years of age, Robert had a deep interest in flying airplanes for the past 15 years. He was, no doubt, an interesting man. There was nothing about Robert that I didn't admire. And, of course, he wanted to have sex, as did I.

The following night was the make-or-break moment. I invited him to dinner at my apartment. I prepared spaghetti, which was easy, but pretty daring for an Irish girl providing dinner for an Italian boy. He actually enjoyed the meal, so after we finished, it was time to approach the relationship.

"Robert, I need to ask you something. We've been going out — ah — four times now, and I am beginning to fall in love with you. Before either of us gets hurt, I want you to know that my goal is to get married. I don't want to waste time in this relationship if that's not where you are."

Certainly, I took Robert by surprise. Four dates didn't seem like enough time even for me. His response, "Is this an ultimatum?" made me answer, "No, this isn't an ultimatum, of course." I really didn't know what he meant by that word but I kept control. "It is, however, a statement of where I want to be headed." Speaking out, saying what I wanted out loud gave me courage. Although I would have been sad if he had walked away, I knew I truly spoke at the right time.

"I'm falling in love with you, too, Aggie. I do want to marry again, and I'd like to work on it with you." This meant we had an exclusive relationship. We would spend time with each other. I would get to know the girls better, and it was time to develop our sexual relationship. I loved Robert's body, and I lusted for his touch, his whole being. What complete joy this relationship was becoming! Within two weeks, Robert formally proposed, and four weeks later, we were married on October 4, 1974, two months before my deadline.

Helen, of course, gave her approval after she came down to check Robert out. My brother John, a young priest, was excited to perform the ceremony. My brothers, Joe and Leo, made plans to celebrate with us. None of my sisters, however, volunteered to come. They could not understand this relationship happening so quickly and counseled me to wait. Worst of all was the letter I received from my mother. Her message was clear as her words burned through the paper.

"How could you do such a thing to me? You, a nun, marrying a divorced man. You'll be sorry trying to raise someone else's children. You mark my words."

My mother was very religious and very righteous, yet I could not believe that she would say these words, much less write them. Should I have been this naïve? She was certainly being true to her past responses to my siblings' engagements, marriages, and divorces.

When Leo got married in 1954, Mother told Leo that he was marrying the wrong girl. Could it have been this attitude that made us all so late for Leo's wedding? Did she deliberately set out to embarrass the bride and groom, or to make them wait for her? If she did, she was fooled because they did not wait. The ceremony had begun. Luckily, it was a Catholic wedding. Otherwise, it would have been over by the time we got there.

Mother then tried her very best to break up my brother Joe's relationship with his serious high school love after he went to Germany with Uncle Sam. When Mary Clare came home very excited with her engagement ring in 1957, Mother, who had already retired for the evening, expressed no interest. Mary Clare's fiancé was downstairs with our dad and engaged in happy conversation. Mother made no effort to join them.

Perhaps this attitude prompted my sister Maureen and her husband, Jim, to secretly elope and not announce their wedding for three weeks. When she did arrive home with the news, Mother lost her temper and her composure so badly that Dad had to call the doctor for something to calm her down, plus our pastor, whom Maureen had informed about the wedding, to assuage her embarrassment.

I knew this history, and like my other siblings, I ignored it. I did not care. No one would force me to give up my Robert, this good, strong, loving man who respected and cared for me and whom I wanted to marry.

We planned a simple wedding on October 4, a Friday night. I asked Barry Roach's wife, Julie, to help me look for a wedding dress. We didn't have much time, so it had to be available immediately and to fit perfectly. This was a new experience for me at 36 years of age, and Julie was a great help. I asked Helen Moye to be my matron-of-honor. She could come down a couple of days before the wedding, but I couldn't wait for her guidance for wedding plans. Robert had introduced me to one of his dear women friends, Gail Randall, who also worked at Martin Marietta, but I did not know her very well at that time. I chose a simple long, knit, white dress with a jacket. No froufrou for me, and no veil.

Although Mother had her tirade, my brothers convinced her that she had to come to Orlando to the wedding. My brother Joe accompanied her, and they arrived on Thursday. Dad said they could not afford to send both. No matter how badly Mother treated each of us as we were preparing to get married, she always seemed to come around as long as we stood our ground and denied her any opportunity to insult our partner. My brother Leo also flew in with his ten-year-old daughter, Terri.

Helen, her husband Henry, and my brother Johnny came to town on Wednesday. Johnny was to perform the ceremony with a Nuptial Mass, so we all drove over to Holy Trinity rectory to meet the pastor with whom we had made arrangements and to see the church. We previously began our celebration at lunch, so we were all feeling mighty fine. Johnny was not dressed in his priestly garb, so there was some hesitancy on the part of the Floridian priest about whether he was the real thing. Johnny showed his identity, as did we.

I suppose the smell of liquor on all of us did not delight the Reverend Pastor. We made arrangements for the wedding rehearsal the following evening at 7 p.m. As the evening approached, Johnny and Robert spent some time together getting to know each other. Johnny felt it was his job as priest, and as representative of the family, to pass his approval on Robert. Robert passed with respect.

The rehearsal evening held special memories. Helen decided we would have a rehearsal dinner for everyone from out of town. She would prepare a turkey dinner, so off to the market we went in late morning. Helen used cream of chicken soup with her turkey that we neglected to pick up, so she sent Henry and Johnny off to buy it at 2 p.m. At 6 p.m,, they returned. They had been to several bars along the way. It looked like there would be no dinner following the rehearsal, but Helen was insistent that she would have it and she wanted no help. At 11 p.m., and after much drinking, we were ready to eat. Although my mother was anxious, she held up throughout, and she had many stories to tell Dad. My friend, Mary Gilbert Kulpinski, and her husband, Joe, arrived with a case of champagne just in time for dinner.

The next day, I had the usual appointments for hair and nails, but that and the wedding cake were the only things normal about this wedding. Robert had the job with Johnny to set up the table and chairs for the reception. It was very informal with appetizers, lots of liquor, and a three-tiered wedding cake. I love wedding cakes, especially if they are white with coconut buttercream icing. All invitations to the wedding were issued informally to Robert's friends and my fellow workers. We had no idea how many to expect.

Robert and I decided we would enter the church together. We wanted to start this journey hand in hand. We were thrilled to have Johnny perform the ceremony because he provided the intimacy of knowing us. His presence banished all the doubts that friends and family may have had about such a short courtship.

The reception at Robert's home was very crowded. We were excited that so many people showed up to celebrate with us. By 9 p.m. we headed for the honeymoon suite at the top of the Holiday Inn in Orlando. On Saturday we left for a brief weekend honeymoon to New Smyrna Beach, a wedding present from one of Robert's fellow workers who owned the condo where we stayed. The universe seemed to churn for us. I believe all of this to be part of God's providence.

For the record, we've been married 48 very happy years. You may wonder how I remember so clearly the details of the early days of our relationship. I wrote a book in 2000 called *The Marriage Plan: How to Marry Your Soul Mate in One Year or Less.* It is available from Amazon in hardback published by Broadway Books of Random House. The book has much more detail if you are interested.

CHAPTER NINETEEN

The Best Laid Plans

WHY WOULD I WANT TO GO TO TEXAS? This was only October and I had just moved twice since July. The last seven weeks had been quite hectic. Actually, this whole year has been a challenge. Could I take one more major change in my life?

One week after Robert and I got married, he was offered a job in Greenville, Texas, with his former company, Boeing. Boeing had taken on a sub-contract with the United States Government called the E4B.

Boeing asked Robert to be the on-site manager at E-Systems, ensuring it was on budget, on schedule, and done according to Air Force specifications. This job was a substantially greater challenge and much more interesting than his work at Martin Marietta. Of course, he should take it.

Mary was a senior in high school, and wouldn't she want to finish with her friends and classmates? Taking out the map, we found that Greenville, Texas, was very rural. It was 60+ miles from Dallas. Not near enough that we could enjoy the benefits and entertainment of the city. Would I be able to work in Dallas, or would the commute be too much? After some thought, I concluded that this could be an opportunity to start my own business. If we could live somewhere in-between Greenville and Dallas, it might work. I prayed for patience, for inspiration, telling Jesus that I knew He had been providing for me. But was this something He really wanted?

It was only after this offer from Boeing that Robert and I both became aware that rumblings of layoffs were in the air in both our departments. If this were the case, God was providing again. Robert and I might both be laid off if we stayed.

I struggled with another issue. Was I being fair to my new bosses? How would Barry, who enticed me to join the company, respond to this news of my leaving after such a short time? What did I owe Martin Marietta?

Both Barry and Winter knew that I wanted to get married. They convinced me that I would find a husband at Martin Marietta. And I did. But none of us had crystal balls. Or maybe we did. Was Robert's offer the fortune teller's response? Were we lucky to get this offer before the news of layoffs broke? Barry and Winter took this news with the genuine graciousness that they always had shown.

Yet we were concerned about Mary. How would she cope in a new high school for her last semester? Mary was disappointed, but her spirit of acceptance of the move gave us courage. Gina seemed ready for a new adventure and excited about going to Texas. We weighed all these considerations with each other and with the girls. Our collective decision was that Robert would take the job. We were all hopeful that this would work for us.

Divine Providence is important to me, but I have to do my part. I have to be clear about what I want. Deep down in my spirit, I wanted to find the right husband more than I cared whether he was divorced or not. My provident God took care of that. I was never sure whether I wanted children or not. So many of my first cousins on my father's side had Down Syndrome children. At 36 years of age, what would be the chance that I would have one? Would I raise whatever child God gave me with love? Now was my chance to prove that. Was I capable of loving Robert's children?

Robert's start date was approximately a month away. We would spend only five weeks together before he would leave Mary, Gina, and me together in Orlando while he searched for a home in Texas. This was not going to be easy for the girls. They had only known me for less than two months, and they had opened their home to me. Since Robert and the girls had moved to Orlando, Mary had stepped up to help her dad with the cooking and keeping the house in order. I sensed she was relieved to have me take over the running of the house during this time, but I needed both Gina's and her help. They had their schoolwork; I had my job.

In the beginning of a marriage, the excitement of being in love as well as the chemistry and lust between two people shock us into the first stages where joy and happiness abound. But what was there to help Mary and Gina accept this intruder, me, into their family? What deep value could bind the kids and me?

Certainly, this was not easy for the girls. As the adult in a house with two teenage girls who had their own rules before I arrived, how should I handle this? They loved their father and respected him, and when it came down to doing what he expected, they had interactive patterns that worked for the three of them. Uncomfortable with my new role as the parent responsible for two teenage girls who had both a mother and a father (with neither present), I felt alone without Robert. I knew I had the role of a wife. But who else was I? I had to just slide into finding out.

Robert understood that I had plenty of experience with teaching teenagers and several degrees in education. Loving the teens I taught during my convent years seemed to be in my DNA. Being with kids aged 13 to 18 gave me great joy. Robert trusted me to work out my role as parent. He also insisted that the children had to listen to and respect what I did and said, a step so many biological parents find difficult to do.

The three of us loved Robert and we knew deep in our hearts, each in our own way, that he had created a good unit for us. What trust he had placed in all of us! It was up to us to honor this trust and to make a real family life. As the adult in our relationship, it was more my responsibility than the girls to make our life together happy and meaningful. And so I began. I suspected that God was preparing all of us for a better relationship by throwing us together when Robert left for Texas.

I brought Sasha, my eight-pound toy Manchester Terrier, into my new home. Mary had both a tabby cat, Tigger, and Benji, a male Lhasa

Apso. The dogs got along, but the cat did not. Sadly, Mary had to find a home for Tigger before our move. Sasha was a dominant male with Benji. Actually, everyone was dominant with Benji. Whenever anyone would correct him, Benji would lie on his back with his feet projecting straight up in the air and urinate all over himself. The messy result made us less the disciplinarians with Benji than we normally should have been. The first time I saw his performance, I stood silent, then I laughed. Then the girls laughed, and Mary started the clean-up process.

In the six weeks that Mary, Gina, and I spent without Robert, I learned much about this new family in my life. They missed their brother, Robbie, and their sister, Michelle. Gina regaled me with stories of the games she and Robbie played, or the way they defended each other when the neighbor kids attacked one of them. Mary, five years older than Gina, filled me in on their mom and home before Orlando- and what it was like for all the children before the divorce. As it is with all deteriorating marriages, it was an unhappy time for the children. The last two years of separation only made Mary long more for little Michelle. She was ten years older than Michelle and often took care of her baby sister whom she wanted back in her life. Divorce is ugly, especially for children, and I was determined that they would never have to endure that pain with me.

I began to sense the role I might take in this new family. A Momma Bear emerged as I grew protective of them. My love for them grew in these six weeks. I felt that God was in control of these massive changes that came upon me since General Motors had laid me off. No doubt it was GM's financial problems that allowed me to begin my new life. Now married with children, I became a firm believer in Divine Providence — and in Helen's marriage plan.

After two weeks of looking for homes, Robert found the one that he thought we would all like. After Thanksgiving, I flew back with him to check out the house. It was the perfect Texas ranch with four bedrooms, a living room, a dining room, and a family room right off the kitchen. If one had any objection, it was the huge back yard filled with globs of "black gumbo" as the Texans called it. When it rained, the dirt stuck to my shoes, and it was quite a task to scrape it off as I stood at the door before entering the house. Something would definitely have to be done about the backyard.

Otherwise, the house was perfect if we were able to negotiate with the builder. Robert's home in Orlando had not yet sold, so the down payment was a problem. I had extraordinarily little savings to help out. Luckily the builder agreed to rent the new house to us until Robert's home was sold. Robert took pictures, and the girls were excited and began to choose their bedrooms. Of course, their solution was to put a pool in that back yard of gumbo. That would have to wait.

Although the girls also missed Robert, they were caught up in preparing for the move as they finished up on their schoolwork. Mary stayed until the middle of January with a friend to be able to finish her semester before she joined us in Rockwall.

CHAPTER TWENTY

Our Family Life Together Begins

GINA, ROBERT, AND I LOADED UP THE 1972 CHEVY IMPALA, and for two days, drove along the 1,000 miles of freeway from Orlando, Florida, to Rockwall, Texas, arriving there on December 23 — just in time to greet the moving van. The movers unloaded the boxes, beds, and clothes. Luckily we easily found the pillows, sheets, pillowcases, and blankets and prepared ourselves for a good night's rest.

That December was freezing in Rockwall. We left warm and beautiful Orlando with the sun shining above and no sweaters, boots, and heavy wool jackets to drag on and off. But it did not deter 13-year-old Gina from making the best of it.

While Robert continued to work on the kitchen, Gina decided that we had to have a Christmas tree. We knew our pickings would be limited on Christmas Eve in the late afternoon, yet we ventured out to tiny downtown Rockwall. The town square had a large county courthouse in the center with small, local stores and offices surrounding that square. We lucked out at the Seven-Eleven. The spruce wasn't very large, but it would fit in the tree stand that we had dug out earlier. We found the Christmas ornaments in their containers, and we were ready to decorate, prepare some hot chocolate, and enjoy Christmas Eve in our new home.

GETTING ADJUSTED

Rockwall was the smallest town in the smallest county in Texas. People were proud of their cattle and farming background. Many girls graduating from high school in the seventies got diamond rings and set dates for their weddings. Boys spoke of wrestling cows and were proud of their redneck attitudes. How would Gina fit in with these southwestern teens?

It so happened that Gina loved animals. She told me the story about several rabbits she had raised when she was only eight. She and her dad built a hutch for the furry creatures. When her Rockwall school needed someone to take home the pet rat that they had in the classroom, Gina volunteered. Not particularly fond of having a rat in our home, I held my ground until Gina convinced me that the rat had a cage and would not get out. She promised to feed and care for him. I wanted Gina to be happy, so Socrates joined our family.

Another name for a Manchester Terrier is a rat terrier. Sasha was living with a rat, and the smell overwhelmed him. He so wanted to get into Gina's room, turning in circles as he tried to get our attention to let him through that door. One day after school, Gina was alarmed that the rat could not be found. Now in spite of my insistence that the rat not come out of the cage, of course Gina would take him out and play with him, cuddling and petting good ole Socrates. She looked and looked for him before announcing with great trepidation that he was lost. I had the solution.

"You know Sasha was bred to find rats; would you like to let him try to sniff out Socrates for you?"

It was a dangerous suggestion for Socrates, but Gina went ahead and allowed Sasha into her bedroom to search. In less than a second, Sasha was snuffling at the plenum underneath the bookcase. Sure enough, Socrates got behind there, but he could not get out. I removed Sasha, closed the bedroom door, and let Gina do the rest. I'm not sure if Socrates ever left the cage again.

Mary had just turned 17 in November before we moved. She seemed to be gifted with maturity that I admired. Not only did she have lovely social skills with an ability to be accepted, but she truly was also magnificently beautiful with skin as soft and white as silk. At 5' 9" with long, flowing blonde hair reaching well below her waist, she adjusted well to finding friends and participating in senior activities. As an "A" student, her acceptance to North Texas State University was no problem.

Everyone in Rockwall seemed to speak with a Texas twang, and "I reckon" and "y'all wanna come on over?" sometimes threw us. A mother of Mary's new friend called and invited us to share some salmon recently caught by her husband in Alaska. This was our first invitation to meet some Rockwall people. But I didn't know whether "y'all" included the children or just Robert and me. So, after stewing for a couple of days, I called back to inquire whether the invitation included the girls. "Oh, no, sweetheart, it's just for us ad~dults." Mary and Gina were not happy. They loved salmon. They were from Seattle. We felt badly they weren't included, but we didn't give up our chance to meet new friends or to have some fresh salmon.

EFFECTS OF DIVORCE ON THE CHILDREN

At the time of his divorce, Robert requested to take all of the children to live with him and was willing to go to court for custody. In the early seventies, the courts demonstrated great bias toward the mother, particularly the Florida courts, and there was very little chance that Robert would win any of the children if he went to court. So he agreed that the younger children, Michelle, 5, and Robert, 10, would live with their mother. Was splitting the family the best choice?

I understood how circumstances force parents to make decisions that work, but we all knew it was bad for the children to be separated. Robert asked me how I felt about getting Michelle and Robbie to live with us. We would contact a lawyer several times, but we were never willing to drag the custody battle into a war. This desire for Michelle and Robbie was so strong in Robert that he tried to get the custody agreement changed, all to no avail. Because it wasn't going to happen, we concentrated on making arrangements for visits to Seattle for us and the girls, and to make an exchange in summer.

During the summer vacations, Michelle and Robbie would come to Dallas for four to six weeks, and Gina would go to Seattle. We had to negotiate away some of our time with Michelle and Robbie so that they could have some time with Gina. Michelle and Robbie were joys to have around. I loved being with them, taking them to swim, or to the movies.

My office was in our home so I could be there for them. As Michelle got older, I took her on my trips to New York where I had some work, or to visit my friend Helen Moye in Flint, Michigan. Robert would take Robbie on trips in his airplane. We truly enjoyed our summers together.

One summer, Robert and I had the opportunity to take Michelle to New York City, and she fell in love with the theater. We saw *Amadeus, Chorus Line,* and *Evita.* By the time we arrived back in Rockwall, Michelle had memorized every song on the *Evita* tape we purchased for her. She was excited to get Frank Langella's autograph after waiting at the stage door for an hour after *Amadeus.*

For several summers, we would drive with the children the thousand miles from Texas to Fort Bragg, North Carolina. Here Robert spent his two weeks of Army Reserve duty attending classes at the John F. Kennedy Special Warfare Center and School. Living in a small, two-bedroom military apartment did not deter the children from having fun. They would swim in the pool, play with other children in the complex, and in general enjoy each other's company with board games. As young Robert entered high school, the time in the summer got shorter for him as he became a dedicated star for the Newport High School football team and returned to Seattle early for practice.

As Robert, the children, and I adapted to our new family, my entrepreneurial spirit surged through my body to give birth to a management training adventure that had been nagging at my brain since getting laid off at General Motors.

A Business for Women's Equality

CHAPTER TWENTY-ONE

Chutzpah, Insolence, Audacity, Impertinence?

WAS IT JUST SIMPLE STUPIDITY TO BELIEVE that I could actually start a management consulting company? Indeed, it took all of the above attributes along with frustration, insecurity, very little money, and a lot of planning. Plus an IBM Selectric typewriter, a landline telephone, a file cabinet, and a Rolodex. Bill Gates and Steve Jobs were relatively unknown as was the world of computers and cell phones. The internet and Wi-Fi were fetuses in 1975. I needed a desk and a chair, but we couldn't afford them, so the kitchen table had to do. A well-supplied office should have pens, pencils, erasers, whiteout, yellow pads, file folders, and those I could pay for. So off I went to the office supply store.

Procrastination always rears its ugly head when we face the unknown, and with the office set-up in the house, I spent time redesigning the furniture layout, mowing the lawn, washing dishes, planning dinner, or grocery shopping. Discipline finally took over when I remembered that I was a goal-setter and I needed a business plan. I got out the yellow pad and began writing out my goals. I wanted to create a management consultant business with training as the emphasis. Management Training — that's what I knew. Teaching was what I enjoyed.

Initially I spent most of the day on the phone with old contacts to get advice on marketing my skills in management education or on restructuring some of the training programs I had worked on at General Motors, the University of Michigan, and Martin Marietta. Having a doctorate in educational administration should help to give me confidence. I should be able to market a basic management training program for supervisors and managers. I was off to the frightening job of making cold calls. Would people hang up on me? Or just laugh at me?

Who would want my services? The telephone yellow pages held a list of corporations large enough to want management training. The "military industrial" complex was certainly represented in the Dallas - Fort Worth area with Texas Instruments, General Dynamics, Vought Corporation, Bell Helicopter, Aerospatiale Helicopter Company, and many smaller companies that fed off them. With my experience at General Motors and Martin Marietta, perhaps they would be open to my ideas. I decided to contact these companies first by calling their training departments to determine their interest. Cold calls scared me, and I hated the thought of making them. Perhaps it was this lack of confidence that came through on the telephone as I inquired of human resource departments if they were looking for outside trainers.

"No, ma'am! We have our training schedule filled," said the receptionist, who was as far as I got on the first phone calls. I then decided to simply ask for an appointment with the Director of Training. If I got the appointment, the answer was the same.

They all seemed to have all the consultants or outside trainers that they needed. I was batting zero. I got the message when a woman who clerked for one of the training departments shared with me, "We only hire men to do our training because so much of it is with the military."

I eventually learned that Martin Marietta's managers were not alone in their bias. These military contractors certainly were not interested in a woman-owned business developing programs for them. They had their "old boy" networks and that was enough. I felt disappointed but not defeated. Actually, I got mad and motivated.

Since Dallas was a regional center for the federal government, I focused on learning about who trained the managers in the Dallas area. The Dallas Office of Personnel Management (OPM) offered management classes for all federal personnel in the five-state region. OPM seemed to be open to anyone who could do the job, and they were looking for help. I was finally in luck.

OPM appreciated my resumé, but they needed to test my training abilities. Could I follow the government manuals? Would I be able to team-teach with OPM staff? My first assignment was to teach a "Management by Objectives" course to highlevel managers in Dallas. I passed the test, and eventually I contracted for several out-of-state classes. My relationship with the OPM Dallas trainers became much stronger after an incident occurred in Louisiana.

One of the trainers at OPM always traveled with me to the state training site. Larry Embrey and I had just finished teaching a class in Alexandria and were headed in my Oldsmobile station wagon (SUV) on Louisiana Hwy 1 to the Shreveport airport where, after dropping off Larry, I would head home to Rockwall.

Darkness fell early in November as we drove north on this country road lined with pine trees. Larry and I were discussing the class when suddenly our conversation was interrupted as we approached a general country store parking lot on the east side of State Hwy 1. It appeared that a black 1939 Pontiac coupe with rounded chassis, fenders, and a rumble seat fading into the shadowy spirit of the night was spitting out red dust and gravel. Accelerating, then braking, the car twisted and turned, each time leaving a cloud of dust in its wake. We were perhaps a hundred yards from the store and the land was free of the pine trees, so I could see pretty clearly. No traffic was in the distance.

Dark and chilly, on that November night only a week from All Hallow's Eve, it was spooky on that road. The driver cycled his wheels south into our lane. As he turned, I spied his dark fedora and then a soft scarf flying out the passenger window. As the car approached, the dust blinded us and I swerved to the opposite lane. The car mirrored my turn and returned with me to my southbound lane. Without looking in the rearview mirror, I grounded my brakes to the floor and coursed through the dust until the road became visible again.

There was no car, no general store, and no parking lot. Larry was not speaking, and the hoary frost had faded his skin to gray. My blouse was drenched with sweat. Our noses burnt from the smell of rubber, and the stench lingered on my lips. We both saw the car. It was no illusion, no gossamer image. Something was there, but what was it?

We drove on to the airport in silence. As Larry opened the car door at the drop-off, I heard, "If you ever tell this story, I'll deny it." I drove the remaining 150 miles west on I-20 toward home, full of fear about what else I might encounter. After telling my story to my husband, he could not wait to verify the story with Larry as he insisted on accompanying me to OPM the following Monday. The office staff in turn anxiously wanted to verify the story with me since Larry could not keep that secret. From that day forward, Larry and I had a special bond. Of course, we were teased, but I always felt it was with respect.

CHAPTER TWENTY-TWO

My Woman Mentor

L UCK CAME MY WAY when I taught a class of directors from various government agencies in Dallas. Helen Killgo, who directed the Work Incentive Program (WIN) at the Department of Labor in Dallas, was impressed with the class she attended and asked me to arrange an appointment with her. The WIN Program, ADC (Aid to Dependent Children), helped women to get back on their feet through job training. Childcare and transportation were giant issues for these women. No less was their need for self-confidence.

As Helen Killgo and I got more acquainted, she arranged for me to train some managers on small contracts. As Regional Director of WIN, Helen had responsibility for training state staffs who operated the programs in their states. My miles on American Airlines built up as I traveled to Austin, Baton Rouge, Little Rock, Oklahoma City, Santa Fe, and cities in between. It was inspiring to work with these state directors who were dedicated to assisting women and children to improve their lives. In many ways, I felt like I was doing God's work, helping those on the margins.

Helen also spread the word throughout the Dallas Department of Labor that they may want to use me for some of their management training. The Job Corps office hired me to train their managers; as a result, my company, J-DL (Jordan-DeLaurenti, Inc.), trained managers at a number of Job Corps Centers throughout the southwest region. I learned from Helen Killgo that a mentor is very important to younger women. Without Helen, my life would have been very different.

I loved training government managers. A general stereotype had existed (and probably still does) that government workers were lazy, had cushy jobs, and couldn't be fired. No doubt the government employees had protections from their unions and other employee organizations against any harm from their managers, but they were as intelligent and engaged in learning as those I had taught in corporations. They seemed to thrive on innovative ideas, and they were motivated to gather the educational credentials to move up in their careers. In addition, most of them felt they were serving their country. They were loyal, patriotic citizens.

One exception always seems to prove the stereotype. I taught a number of management classes for supervisors in a federal department in Dallas. At Christmastime, I dropped off a not-very-expensive box of chocolates to each of the managers who hired me. Most of them thanked me and passed it around to their people. The head-honcho returned it to me in the mail with a note that they did not accept gifts from vendors. I figured that it simply wasn't big enough because his actions were so insulting. A gift of candy for the department was not forbidden by the Federal Bribery Statue governing public officials.

By the end of 1977, I had increased my business. The income was enough for me to hire a part-time secretary, but not large enough to provide a decent salary to help support my new family. Barbara Bugg, a tall, good-looking blonde with amber glass frames whose son, Mike, and our Gina were friends, answered my ad in the local Rockwall paper. Barbara was intelligent and a college graduate who just wanted a part-time job while caring for her two children and her husband. Our needs complemented each other. She wanted something to do, and I needed her talent, her generosity, her honesty, and her flexibility.

Barbara had a key to the house and would work her own time schedule when I was out of town. One summer day she entered the house when we were all out of town. As she opened the door, zillions of fleas attacked her. The dogs were in a kennel, but unknown to us, fleas had been nesting on them and now were throughout the house. Barbara took control, bought a few flea bombs, set them off, and quickly left the house. Often I was overwhelmed at how lucky I was to have Barbara willing to work with me. This was certainly one of those times. Most people would have closed the door and never returned.

SBA AND J-DL

In order to grow the business, I needed to be able to compete for larger contracts. Government rules required competitive bidding for contracts over $10,000. Procurement departments out of Washington D.C. were responsible for these contracts, and it was very difficult to break the good-ole-boy network. Helen Killgo suggested that I should be doing longer term contracts, which was better-paying work. This meant competing for the contracts with much larger programs and against competitors a hundred times my size. The problem was that I did not have the finances to demonstrate that I could do those contracts on a large scale."The large companies will eat you alive," Helen said. "You need to get on the list of SBA 8(a) contractors." This was 1977, two years after we worked with her department.

What Helen Killgo did not know was I could qualify at once as financially disadvantaged. Robert's salary minus child support for two children barely put us above the poverty level, much less allowed us to get a start-up business underway. The history of my father's struggle with raising seven children after World War II, when the mafia put him out of business in Pennsylvania, was another reminder.

Soon I was digging into research on the program. Although the program initially targeted African American males, under Parren Mitchell, a congressman from Maryland, the language of the bill did not limit it to them. All minorities were to be included, yet only five minority females had been admitted to the program by 1975, eight years after it had begun.

Congressman Mitchell did not budge when, through Ralph Hall, my Congressman from Rockwall, I got a private appointment with Mitchell and presented my case. Congressman Mitchell passionately said to me, "This program is for African Americans and maybe other minorities, but not for white women." I was not only disappointed but incredibly angry at what I saw as a grave injustice. If I were in the program, I would not have deprived any minority of participating. I believed, as did Helen Killgo, the contracting pie was large enough for all of us.

No doubt the white male network was upset that they now saw their extraordinary share reduced by the African American males, in spite of the fact that the white male network still controlled 99% of the procurement dollars in the federal agencies. The fight against women, and I thought me in particular, was closing in on all sides. I reached out to every name I could find to give me information. I visited some of the local SBA staff, one of whom gave me a list of approved 8(a) contractors. After calling all the names on that list and leaving a message, not one returned my calls.

Undaunted, or just motivated by the unfairness I encountered, I made an application through the Dallas SBA office. I expected the director, a woman, to be sympathetic to my plea. Not all women support other women. She rejected my application, echoing Congressman Mitchell. I appealed to the national SBA 8(a) Assistant Secretary in Washington D.C. The rejection was firm. This program was not for white women, especially married ones. Helen Killgo disagreed. She was determined that I did not give up.

Initially, the SBA rejected my efforts to apply because I was not "socially and economically disadvantaged." I later had learned through records procured under the Freedom of Information Act that this female director lied during the meetings concerning my application, claiming that it was my husband who wanted to run the company and was putting me up to this. She declared that he was a retired full-time Army Colonel getting a pension which I did not declare on my application.

I did not declare a pension because there was none. In addition to working for Boeing, Robert was an active member of the Army Reserves since 1957. He had just been promoted to Colonel, an unpaid position. The director also declared the program was not for white women, especially married white women, no matter whether they qualified in all other categories. Although these statements fueled my anger when I read what she had said, the bias proved to be helpful later.

Through my library searches, I learned that the SBA had settled a lawsuit with Marilyn Andrulis, PhD, a woman out of Washington D.C., to admit her into the 8(a) program. SBA was careful to admit Dr. Andrulis on a set of criteria that applied only to her and did not cover other women, white or black. I contacted Marilyn Andrulis, and soon I was on my own path to a lawsuit. Marilyn became my guide through this process, introducing me to her lawyer who introduced me to another lawyer who was willing to take my case.

The SBA feared any discussions with, or applications from, any white woman. An attitude prevailed that any woman married to a white man would be a front for the male. They were determined to give credence to the stories reported in newspapers about white males who used their wives to obtain SBA grants and loans in some recently established federal programs. I'm not sure how many of those were true, but I know the white men were red-faced angry that minorities and women were getting some of their procurement pie. Those in SBA decision-making roles acted and spoke as though all married white women were fronts for their husbands.

Women were having a tough time getting financial help despite the new federal banking statutes. In addition, newspaper articles reported that minority males were also fronting for white male partners. I would never be anybody's front, not only because I highly valued truth, but also because of my pride, determination, and independent spirit.

Seeking Other Avenues of Business

During the nearly three years of this SBA battle, I sought out other possibilities to grow the business. One large contract that kept J-DL alive was with an oil company in east Texas. The top executives there recognized that their managers had little motivation to hire, train, and supervise minorities and females because of the prejudice that characterized their daily lives.

The company had contracted with Tom, an African American consultant, who owned a company out of Stone Mountain, Georgia. Tom learned about my previous work with women's programs and recommended that this Fortune 100 company hire me to collaborate with him to achieve their goals of assimilating women and minorities into their culture. The strategy was to start the program with managers and the union leaders, almost all of whom were white males. This became an overwhelming challenge considering the employees in this Texas city were deeply entrenched in the white culture of the South.

For two years, I traveled two weeks out of every month and would return home at the end of those weeks with pounding headaches. Prejudice was not hidden. People said what they believed. We heard stories of fellow workers putting sugar in the gas tanks of black union workers, of women being constantly harassed verbally and sexually by both managers and fellow workers. It was not only the blue-collar workers but also highly educated chemical engineers, sophisticated research analysts, and MBA graduates who suffered daily insults and isolation. We saw the need for the company's desire to train, but the managers had to change their own belief systems before they would change their behavior, and that was a struggle for them.

My first morning at the refinery, a high-level manager was given the job of escorting me to the training area. This manager was easily 6', with a joyful and garrulous personality. He made me laugh and I enjoyed his greeting. We began our tour with his taking his arm and putting it around my shoulder. With a great deal of discomfort and instant reaction, I took his arm off, looked into his face and said, "This will be our first lesson." We continued on without any further discussion until our class began. He was a very willing learner.

Tom and I experienced the hatred that racial prejudice and gender discrimination promotes. We were warned by a union leader, one who assisted us in the workshops, that the two of us should not be seen alone, particularly riding in a car together, going out to a restaurant, or socializing in any way, especially after dark. He offered to go with us or to give us his shotgun to defend ourselves. We rejected the offers, but it was not without fear.

One evening, we drove out to a restaurant that had freshly caught oysters, shrimp, and crayfish. It was "crawfish" season in the bayou. The restaurant had wooden benches and white butcher paper covering the red-painted picnic tables so we could dig into those shells and discard them with abandon. A lot of work but worth it. We were hungry and our conversation was filled with descriptions of those succulent dishes we were awaiting. Finally, the seafood arrived, and we dug in.

Shortly thereafter, several young fathers dressed in gimme caps and assorted colors of sports jackets led their nine- and ten-year-old, base-ball-uniformed sons behind them as they piled into the booth across from us. Soon one father, quite loudly pointing us out in language that should have been forbidden in the restaurant, was telling the entire restaurant how wrong it was for us to be there together, with emphasis on a black man and a white woman.

Tom and I, both more stubborn than the average water buffalo facing a pride of lions, stayed longer at the table that night than we would have ordinarily. We deliberately ordered refills on our beer and delayed before ordering our dessert. We continued our conversation, showing no signs of our discomfort. We were determined to make them uncomfortable in their own satanic passion. Leaving the restaurant, however, we showed less courage. I kept careful watch inside the restaurant door while Tom went to the parking lot for the car.

"Lady," I heard behind me, "you're a disgrace, N*&%#*-lover." Tom looked at me as I buckled up saying, "Maybe we should have taken that shotgun."

This experience convinced us that we would not let fear change our behavior in or out of the classroom, for that was exactly what many hoped would happen. We had a chance to change a culture. Many of the union workers and a few of the managers wanted us to go away. We stayed two years because we both needed the money, the company executives recognized their need for deep and lasting change, and the women and minority employees told us that the refinery and the chemical plant managers were finally getting the message.

As satisfying as the money and success were, I had no regrets about moving on when finally, late in 1979, the SBA succumbed to the brilliant pressure of my lawyer from the Women's Legal Defense Fund. Linda Schneider was my David to the SBA's Goliath and had graduated first in the same law school class where their Goliath finished near the bottom. We won. I was admitted to the SBA 8(a) program. And I celebrated the award of my first large federal contract with the Department of Labor, WIN program, led by Program Director Helen Killgo. Without my mentor, it would not have happened.

CHAPTER TWENTY-THREE

Husband Signs or No Loan?

I HAD DIFFICULTY TRYING TO GET A LOCAL BANK to support my efforts to grow. My little company had been in utero long enough. It was time for its birth. But for that, I needed a midwife, a bank. I approached the president of my bank in Rockwall, Texas, with a business plan and an application for a small loan. Everything was small: my company, my loan request, my bank, and even the president's stature with tiny eyes behind his large, dark eyeglass frames and a Rockwall accent as evident as his "old boy beliefs."

Rockwall Bank was built on a farm and ranch culture. The bank was so trustful of all the citizens that they placed counterchecks at retail shops that did business with them. In my early days in Rockwall, I went to pick up my clothes at Jerry's cleaners and forgot my cash and my checkbook. It didn't matter. On the counter was the bank checkbook.

"You got an account with the bank?" Jerry muffled.

"Sure," I responded in my East Coast directness.

"Then go ahead, honey, just write yourself a check."

That really meant write him a check. I was reluctant, but sure enough, it was no trouble. The check went through.

I opened a bank account for my business with the bank when I first started in 1975. Robert and I both had a joint account. It was time for me to gain the bank's support for several contracts I had signed. It would take some money to get me through at least the first month or two, before I would get paid. Everything in the loan package was acceptable except for the fact that my husband's signature was absent. The bank president told me without apology, "Honey, I can't give a married woman a loan without her husband's signature. My Board of Directors would never allow that."

With my eyes staring straight at him, and my mouth paralyzed for a moment, I stuttered, "You don't mean that, Jake. That's against the law."

I was not an unknown. The bank had our account. I and about five other women had started the League of Women Voters local chapter in Rockwall. I was the president, and we had an account there. Having conducted some seminars for a few organizations in Rockwall, I had received some publicity in the local paper that the president's dear friend owned. I was gobsmacked, but suddenly, I gained control. Not a good thing. I set out to convince the president those banks are required to follow the Equal Credit Opportunity Act of 1974.

"Jake, are you familiar with the Equal Credit Opportunity Act of 1974?"

I got no answer, so I continued. "It's only three years old, but it says that banks have to provide equal treatment to women seeking credit."

Oh, his shoulders straightened, his cheeks puffed, and he got angry. "What kind of marriage do you have anyway? I don't understand that you don't want to get your husband's support?"

Furious at this question, yet I needed to stay in control. So, I answered with my Cheshire cat grin, "Now, Jake, honey, you know you can't ask me that question."

After four years I could "honey" with the best of them. At this point I was only asking for $10,000, and I had enough business to more than support the payback.

"Robert's not involved in the business. My marriage should have nothing to do with the loan." I continued but in a much more congenial tone. I knew the law. I did my research. "If I were single, you would give me that loan. Yet you are telling me that in Rockwall, in 1979, married women need their husband's signature? Oh, Jake, I know you don't want to break the law."

I did not tell him that I knew that the culture, and sometimes the Texas laws, still asserted that women needed their husband's permission to make financial decisions. With less intensity, I asked, "Jake, please explain to me the need for that requirement since the law forbids it."

He was silent. So I went on. "I have all the collateral necessary for that loan with these contracts that I have attached."

He reacted, "The Board requires a husband to sign."

I responded,

"Jake, would you tell the Board that I own and run the business. My husband has no interest or ownership in this business. I am committed to this business full-time, and I want to grow it. You know, I know, and they know, they cannot require this. The law is on my side. Would you do that for me, please?"

The Board of Directors would meet on Saturday morning, and Jake was not willing to present my application as-is. As Anne Richards, Governor of Texas, often said, "This dog was not going to hunt, so figure out a way that the cow ate the cabbage." So I got this idea:

"Jake, I'm going to ask you a big favor. I need you to give me some quarter with this idea I have. I'm a management consultant, and often we suggest to managers when they meet an impasse that role-playing might help. Would you be willing to let me play a role with you?"

Where did I get this nerve? My God, he was a bank president and a prominent citizen of Rockwall. I was becoming Helen Killgo. As we sat across from each other in his glass-enclosed cage inside the bank entrance, I offered,

"I would like you to pretend that you never met me, and I'm going to go out the door and come in as a single woman with this proposal in hand. There's no Robert, no marriage. Just me. I would like you to read it while I'm here, as a single woman. Take your evaluation sheet and do your analysis. If you still believe that I am not a good risk, I'll accept your decision."

Much to my amazement, Jake agreed. Perhaps no one had ever asked him to perform before. Or had I weighed him down and he just wanted to get rid of me? I picked up my proposal, placed it back in my case, walked out the front door — not only of his office but of the bank entrance. I walked back in, knocked on his door, and introduced myself while shaking his hand across the desk.

"I'm Aggie Jordan. Four years ago I moved here to Rockwall to start my business. I've been a client of this bank for these four years."

Jake was intrigued. He stood up to greet me and shook my hand. He was playing the role as I requested. I sat down, took the proposal out of my attaché case, and handed it to Jake. I fluttered between defeated and powerful for 20 minutes as I waited silently for him to finish the task. He was reading every word and took a calculator to the numbers.

Finally, Jake looked up with surprise and chagrin, "I still don't think the Board are male chauvinists. I'll make the presentation to them."

I never mentioned the words "male chauvinists," but evidently, he got the message. He got to the heart of the issue. He was subtly admitting that it was chauvinistic to demand my husband sign the loan proposal. I thanked him for his patience and consideration and for being such a good sport, adding that it was important to me that he understood what I was trying to say.

On Monday I received a call from Jake to tell me that the Board approved my loan. I decided that, when I went to the bank for my check, I would tape the conversation. The previous encounters I had with chauvinists made me mistrust Jake and the Board.

I entered the office with my tape recorder turned on in the attaché case. I admit this was ethically questionable, but I really did not trust what other obstacles Jake might put in my way. I remembered with some tremor how the president at Lewis University had secretly taped our deans' meetings when the recorder alarm went off at the end of the tape. I was hoping that didn't happen to me.

In my previous conversation, I had mentioned to Jake that he could not ask me questions about my husband, but Jake was still hesitantly curious and persistent. After we finished the paperwork and he handed me the check, he said, "We're finished with business now, right?" I agreed. He continued, "Do you mind if I ask you what kind of marriage you have?"

I had the check, but I still had to pay it off and continue my relationship with the bank. Where the following response came from, I will never know, but I answered, "Oh, Jake, I have a very traditional marriage."

I couldn't get out of there fast enough, but Jake wanted to keep on talking. I offered him my hand, "Thank you, Jake. I'm sorry I must run. I have another appointment. I am really grateful for this loan."

When I got home, Robert was anxious to hear that recording. His response after listening was, "What's a traditional marriage anyway?" Beats me.

I wonder if Jake ever entertained with that story. I know I got plenty of fodder out of that role-play.

This loan was the beginning of a long relationship of small loans with Rockwall Bank. In 1986, I appeared as a witness before the Congressional Banking Committee on the progress women were not making in securing credit. I sat before this committee and told my story with Jake and Rockwall Bank. Congressman Ralph Hall was at the Committee hearing and asked me, "Jake really said he couldn't give you a loan because you were a woman?" I knew Ralph had previously been on the Rockwall Bank Board and knew those officers very well, so I wondered if I was now to be on the hotseat.

I was shaking in my red St. John suit and three-inch heels — until I heard, "Well, congratulations, I'm glad you got that loan. Next time, if you have a problem, call my office."

After the meeting, the Congressman asked me to meet him in the bar of the Madison Hotel at seven that evening with his chief of staff. He wanted to hear about my business and what he could do to help me. For the first time in all my struggles, I felt like someone was listening to my situation and appreciated the battles that I as a woman-business owner had. Congressman Hall was on the Small Business Administration

Congressional Committee, and I was giving him my stories. I was grateful that J-DL was growing, but growth meant that I needed bank loans to support the multi-million-dollar contracts that I wanted to go after. Congress had empowered the Small Business Administration to guarantee loans up to $500,000, and I told the Congressman and his chief of staff how difficult the SBA policies made it for all of us small businesses, whether male or female. He left the bar that evening after telling the chief of staff to look into the changes that would need to be made to make the process more workable.

I would spend hours, night after night, getting my figures together after having worked all day plus getting our family dinner and getting organized. I had to back up the figures with copies of proposals that we had submitted to government agencies. Preparing the required voluminous paperwork was tedious, but I needed the loan. Getting approval from SBA was a monumental task in spite of the fact that I had SBA 8(a) certification.

The SBA regional office in Dallas knew me well and had all the documentation requested, but they still insisted that I go through an in-depth, exhaustive examination process. It took over 90 days to gather all the information they kept asking for. By the time I handed in the final work, they told me my original application was out of date. I was furious inside, but if I wanted that loan, I had to start the paperwork all over again. It took over two years, in my eighth year of business, for me to successfully acquire my first loan of $500,000. But I kept at it.

CHAPTER TWENTY-FOUR

Misogyny and Growth

MISOGYNY HAS BEEN WITH US, I suppose, since the first humans developed on this earth. And it is still with us. Over those millions of years, the degree has certainly lessened. But that degree has depended on how actively women have engaged in the fight for women's equality.

Many Texas laws declared women to be chattel until 1967, when Attorney Louise Raggio decided to do something about it. Frustrated because her husband had to sign bail bonds for her clients, this 4' 11", 100 lb. lady dynamo helped draft the Texas Marital Property Act of 1967, which gave a woman the right to own property, secure a bank loan, or start a business without her husband's consent. I started my company only eight years later in 1975. Referring to a woman's lack of rights under Texas law prior to 1967, Raggio once said, "It was idiots, convicts, minors, and married women who didn't have property rights."

We women business owners loved Louise Raggio. She was our hero and our mentor in Dallas. We were grateful to her. She gave us courage to do what needed to be done. She had no pretense about her, and with much humor, reminded us to speak up, step forward, and be prepared. She was known and she was heard. She gave me courage to speak up since my company had the ability to change the corporate culture. She recognized that misogyny gave me an opportunity to grow my company. Women in companies were suffering insult and neglect because they were women. I had the experience to help them to succeed in business.

I was spending my time making every effort to be heard by the SBA. Since the struggle was difficult and long, I recognized that the business had to go in another direction. Government contracts were not our only interests. During the three years of battle with the SBA, other doors I previously had knocked on had begun to open.

I had made a cold call on a company we will call XYZ at its regional office in Dallas. Luckily, the woman in charge of training there was open to addressing the issues the company had with keeping women in their sales force. I presented my background with General Motors and Martin Marietta, explaining the programs that I had done to help managers assimilate women into their companies. They were interested and excited, but the training supervisor told me that she had her own system to convince of the need for this training. When I had not heard for several months, I put that effort aside until that woman called to tell me that they had some success. They made the contacts for me with the headquarters on the East Coast. The executives wanted help. I lost no time in making that appointment.

Since I was living in Dallas, I took advantage of the flight east to visit my mother in Pennsylvania. I was going to rent a car and drive to New England. My generous brother Johnny decided to take off a day and drive me. I was excited but nervous about the appointment, but that ride with my brother relaxed me. The meeting went well, and to celebrate, Johnny said, "Let's stop and get some ice cream before we head back." There in Greenwich was this old-fashioned ice cream parlor where we not only ordered delicious milkshakes. Since we didn't have lunch, we ordered two each. This was the first time and the last either of us ever had two milkshakes – for me, one chocolate, one vanilla – and without any guilt. Johnny and I laughed about this the whole way back to Pennsylvania.

XYZ was a godsend, and during these years I began a decade-long relationship with the company. Using my experience, I developed two programs for assimilating and training women in sales for management. We put an all-out effort to capture the attention of male managers as well as women.

XYZ's sales staff had definitive proof that the culture was not supportive of their efforts to retain female new hires. A great deal of money was spent to train salespeople, and they needed to keep them after they were trained. Women were always at the top of the sales ladder, but it was not enough to keep them in the game. Their saleswomen were making plenty of money, but they were not happy. After two or three years, they left XYZ for companies where they found a greater comfort level, often smaller companies that paid less.

My charge was to identify the reasons for these departures and to assist in helping the company retain their successful women. The program took off, and many saleswomen grew successful and happy careers. The program did not solve all of the problems, but it gave the foundation for creating a culture where women could succeed.

The company scheduled our first J-DL sales training to follow a national sales meeting. On the morning we introduced the first class, several of the women told a story about how the sales meeting had ended the day before. At the wrap-up, the leader gave a talk on the necessity of assimilating woman into the sales force. To conclude his speech, he cheered, "Okay, now folks, put your balls to the walls and get out there and sell."

This manager had no idea that it was this kind of systemic corporate language that caused women to feel invisible. This same leader came to our class to welcome the women and to describe how much the company was doing to support them. I couldn't wait to relate this story to that manager and to the executives the first time I trained them.

It was fun and satisfying to see the women identify all the motivations the companies used for their male workforce that isolated the women: golf games for their male co-workers, trips to customers that rarely included the women, gentlemen-only clubs like the Playboy clubs, off-color jokes, denigrating language — "little lady," "the girls," "my girl," or "Girl Friday."

From sales we headed off to manufacturing, which was a greater challenge. We found exceptionally bright, capable women: engineers, MBAs, accountants, and lawyers who were getting great reviews but were not getting promoted. How could they compete with their male counterparts when so much cultural bias existed? The women were ready for this training. So much so that they started to socialize after class. I would join them and hear the stories, as one by one they told of being deprived of a promotion or simply an opportunity to attend a meeting they should be leading because their Japanese customer would not listen to a woman. When this word got up the chain to the highest levels, the company took command. If a woman had the job of leading the customer project, she would be in control, not some stand-in man. If her project meant she had to go to Japan, some male manager would not replace her. The training was beginning to succeed.

When some women pointed out that they had to travel to another building to use a lady's room, managers started to take action. The facilities department was instructed to solve the problems of not enough ladies' rooms and inconvenient placement.

We trained the women to understand the steps they had to take to be successful in their manufacturing environment. How do you become assertive when the manager sees women speaking up for themselves as pugilistic? The women wrote role-plays and practiced being heard. I often used my example of the role-play with the bank president to get the point across. They had to do their homework, presenting their case in a direct and calm manner, to take control of their lives and not give up. Women had been giving up too easily.

These women were bright, and it did not take long for them to change the culture of their own departments. They told their managers what they wanted and asked for guidance to get it. Managers began to recognize the barriers that stood in the way of women getting promoted. These women were fired up to contribute to the company's manufacturing division, and soon their managers recognized that they had to take the time to guide the women to success. From the top down, executives were committed to assure that talented women would be recognized.

Life changed for women and men in the company, and it wasn't long before women started up the corporate structure where even the Chief Executive Officer was not beyond reach. The companies benefited but J-DL did, too.

J-DL's success in one company led to programs with many Fortune 500 corporations as well as universities. In each of these organizations, brilliant women rose to positions of great responsibility. Managers became open to recognizing their talents and to mentoring them. My personal gratitude goes to the women whom I cherished in these organizations. Although the names of many escape my memory, I still have joy when I think of Marie McKee, Maureen Natelli White, and Diane Gulbrandsen. These women guided me through the tsunamis of cultural change in these corporate oceans. Without them, there would have been no success. Each of the women became successful in their own careers.

I found it gratifying to learn that, although there was plenty of male chauvinism around corporate America, a number of male managers were dedicated to eliminating it. These men recognized that they were losing multiple contributions of a sizable percentage of their corporate talent if they continued to allow such bias to exist against women. These men in all corporations deserve credit for changing their cultures. I collaborated with Directors of Training, Vice Presidents of Personnel, Directors of Procurement, and the CEOs of these corporations who took the risk to sponsor these programs. And J-DL profited from the need and the desire of corporations to assure that the talent of women was not wasted.

I am happy to have made this contribution for women. I feel that this work was as sacred as anything I may have done in the past, and we made money — a worthy combination for success.

CHAPTER TWENTY-FIVE

Upturns and Downturns

IN THE SPRING OF 1980, my husband, Robert, finished the contract in Greenville and we were faced with a decision. Would he accept a substantial offer to return to Seattle with The Boeing Company? We would be much better off financially if he accepted, but neither Robert nor I could see the wisdom in giving up the business that I had started and struggled so hard to grow.

Robert's confidence in J-DL and in me was great, but I had some concerns. Could we survive if Robert gave up his salary and came to work for J-DL? Should Robert look for another job in the area?

I needed someone full-time who could relieve me from the back-office responsibilities: accounting, payroll, invoices, and government contracting experience. I was doing the marketing, training, proposal writing, and trying to run the operation. Through these first five years, Robert managed the accounting tasks on the weekend for me. The computer age for small businesses was dawning, and Robert was first to understand what equipment and software J-DL would need to grow.

We were hopeful with the SBA 8(a) certification that my company would be successful, but it had a long way to go. The growth of the women's training programs was demanding more administrative attention. Most entrepreneurs I know find it hard to give up control. I was no exception. In addition, I had the likely burden of SBA or minority contractors now seeing this as Robert's business. So bringing Robert into the business was a risk on so many levels. But risk-averse, I was not. More reason for Divine guidance.

Through the SBA 8(a) certification and Helen Killgo's recommendations to her fellow directors, J-DL began to get a foothold with government contracts. Work with the Department of Labor led to jobs with the employment security departments (better known to most of us as the provider of unemployment checks) in Texas, Arkansas, New Mexico, Louisiana, and the City of Dallas. All these contracts helped the company to grow its business.

SLIDING AWAY

For us, 1982 was the worst recession we experienced. I say this fully recognizing that recessions have their cycles and that many people have battled to survive in 2007-2009 as well as in the economy of 2020-2022 as COVID-19 has raged. People have lost homes, jobs, savings, and a sense of security. But all losses are judged by their personal impact.

We had geared up for a million-dollar contract with the Department of Labor, which had been awarded to us. But before we went into operation, the contract was unilaterally canceled. I had been negotiating with SBA for a loan, believing that I would have needed it for the Labor contract. The economy was in free-fall and so was J-DL. XYZ and ABC Glass canceled their programs. All our contracts were put on hold or canceled except for two.

Money became a profoundly serious issue. There just wasn't enough. We reduced our corporate staff by two-thirds. How does one decide whom to let go and whom to keep? A few saw the writing on the wall and left to find other jobs.

One of our most senior employees indicated in a public meeting that she felt we were not being open with them, and she wanted to see the financials. I looked at Robert, who was shaking his head in disbelief.

She continued, "I will have to give it some serious thought in the next six months whether I want to stay with J-DL." The meeting room was full of tension. There was no rattling of paper or shifting of bodies. All eyes were down in disbelief that this very senior and respected employee would publicly express mistrust. Attacking the owner of the company was not the ticket to continued employment, especially when the CEO was doubtful if J-DL would be alive in six months.

As much anger as I felt at the moment, I wanted to say, "You don't have to wait six months, you can go now." But I didn't. If I had taken that action out of anger and thrown reason out the door with her, I suspected, I would be in more trouble than we already faced. True, employees were as upset and unraveled as much as we were about the downturn in business, and knowing this, I kept my cool and simply defended our position.

Did we communicate the failing conditions clearly? I thought so, but when jobs are threatened, mistrust is one factor that takes control. A few did not believe that we simply did not have any money. In the latter part of 1981, we had purchased a Cadillac. It undoubtedly gave the impression to our employees that we were doing well. And we were, compared to all the previous struggles. We were so proud of that car, a sign of our success. The Cadillac soon became our salvation as an asset we could sell for cash. Although we only received 40 percent of its value, it was enough to pay a payroll for our reduced staff.

For the next payroll, my brother loaned us the money. Not only did both transactions get us through a month of debts and near disaster, but they were injections of energy. Up to that point, we were losing faith. Robert was inquiring about going back to Boeing. Although I never thought of looking for a job, I recognized that I alone would be the company. I would be back on the road traveling.

RECOVERY

At Christmastime, we went to Seattle to visit with Robert's father, who was then 85 years old. One of our managers, Ora Woods, volunteered to cover for our last day away. From the depths of hope came a call from the Federal Aviation Administration (FAA) in Oklahoma City. Could we possibly come and talk to them the following week? Ora did not hesitate to take control. She could drive to Oklahoma City and stay with her mother who lived nearby. Ora and I stayed connected by telephone. She set up the appointment, prepared the government marketing package, and gathered from FAA the information we would need to work with the SBA. By the time I returned to start the new year, we had received a call from the FAA that we were their choice. The good karma for 1983 started to roll.

The work was urgent. FAA was in consternation at this time. Ronald Reagan had earlier fired the striking air traffic controllers. The FAA office in Seattle was being closed, and employee frustration had taken over. The information was necessary in order to transfer the employee personnel records into permanent files, and the FAA in Oklahoma City was given the task.

Luck was on our side with this contract. We hired an Air Force retired Colonel, Lloyd B. McKeethen, to run the program. "Mac" was brilliant, organized, fair, and well respected by the FAA. The program was so successful that it was the beginning of a 12-year contractual relationship with the FAA. Most of the credit goes to Colonel McKeethen. Eventually J-DL was responsible for training FAA ground personnel at the FAA Academy in Oklahoma City. Mac eventually joined us at our offices in Dallas to operate these contracts until he retired after ten years of service with us.

Relief was in sight when SBA finally approved our loan. The length of time it took to get the money made me very uncomfortable. My payment to my brother was way past due. Although it would be another month or two before the money was available, we struggled through and were able to pay back my brother and begin anew.

In addition to hiring Mac McKeethen, another important personnel decision we made in this crisis period was to hire Jeanne Bickford as our Executive Assistant. We were extremely fortunate when Jeanne applied for the job. A psychology major in college, Jeanne had worked as an assistant to a vice president at Frontier Airlines in Denver. She had battled breast cancer at a young age and wanted a job with less stress. Jeanne surmised that working for a small company would be less stressful for her. She would soon learn how unreal that assumption was.

Through the years Jeanne was my bulwark, my twin spirit, who knew what needed to be done sometimes before I did. The company was not less stressful in terms of work, but the atmosphere we tried to create provided us great growth potential for our employees. Jeanne was direct, trustworthy, assiduous until the tasks were complete, and positive through trials as well as successes. I was often concerned that we were putting too much on her, knowing that stress can be a stimulant for cancer. But Jeanne would always say, "This is a different kind of stress. I like it here."

I am sure I was not always easy to work with. My communication was not always as clear as it could be. The balls I had in the air took my attention away from the tasks Jeanne was handling. I made quick decisions and often didn't lay the groundwork for implementing them. I could always count on Jeanne to fill in, ask the questions, and sit me down for some difficult discussions. When she was uncertain, Jeanne would call on Robert for help. Often the two of them would have to gang up on me to set me straight.

When that happened, I knew what was good for me. I listened and acted. Our overall success was as much due to Jeanne, and of course, Robert, as it was to any other factor.

These government programs were dear to my heart, profitable, and demanding. Even though I had to limit the training that I did in the initial stages of the company, I never wanted to stop my contact with the development of women in business and government. Sometimes I would wonder, *How did I get from 14 years as a Catholic nun fully dedicated to teaching, to running a company of 500 people, primarily dedicated to doing business with the United States Government?*

The answer is, of course, we never know in what direction we might evolve. As long as we listen to our inner voice and are willing to take risks, plus open ourselves to learning from whomever and wherever the teacher might be, we can trust in our own guidance system. My compass has always been trusting in Divine Providence. That has not changed from the days of growing up in a Catholic family to my life as an entrepreneur.

CHAPTER TWENTY-SIX

Having My Voice Heard
in Washington

A SUPPORTIVE CONTACT I HAD AT SBA encouraged me to get involved with an upcoming White House Conference on Small Business that would be held in September 1986. "In order to be a delegate to the conference," he told me, "you have to be elected to represent the Dallas SBA Region."

I had never run for anything, nor did I belong to any small business groups that could support me. I was an unknown on the local level. My networking targeted issues around our government business with the National Association of Federal Women Contractors that Marilyn Andrulis founded. I had been fairly ignorant of local small business associations, to say nothing of what existed statewide. The local associations of Women in Construction, the National Association of Women Business Owners (NAWBO), minority businesses contractors, and the local Chamber of Commerce had all selected their representatives to run for election to the White House Conference as representatives from Texas.

How was I going to get elected? My only chance was to go to the local conference and campaign with the attendees. I had to do something to get attention. Our daughter Michelle suggested that I wear a big hat like Minnie Pearl. So together, we decorated a large straw floppy hat with the sales ticket hanging down along with my name, "Aggie."

When the weekend arrived for the local conference, I spent the two days involved in the numerous meetings, spoke up, and campaigned with other independent owners. If I was going to wear this silly hat, then I had to have the courage to walk up to conferees at the convention center and introduce myself.

"Hi, I'm Minnie Pearl and I'm running to be a delegate to the White House conference. I sued the SBA and won." That did it. Someone would say, "You really don't look like Minnie Pearl." I would then give them my real name and tell them, "I want to be sure that we business owners get the banks to loan us money that we desperately need." About everyone I talked to understood that cry. "That's high on my list," one would say. Then another, "How does the SBA help you get loans?" There I was off and talking to them about SBA loans and the barrier that banks put in front of us. One would say, "We need to get laws passed to get small business loans. I need a small loan for $10,000 right now."

Soon people were gathering around me asking questions about their businesses and relating what they needed the money for. When I talked about the women's issues, the gender insults, the downright bias that bankers had for women business owners, women seemed to be very willing to share their stories with all of us. By the time I would get to Washington, I expected to have tens of stories for our meetings and our visits to the congressional offices.

But first I had to win the election. I knew those involved with the associations had their spots locked up. But the Minnie Pearl gambit worked. People remembered me when it was time to vote. I couldn't believe that silly hat got me elected to the 1986 White House Conference.

About twelve of us carried the Dallas Regional banner to Austin to join others elected from each region in Texas. We had to get our issues on the State of Texas platform. This was a competitive, hard-fought give-and-take that prepared us for the bigger battle in Washington D.C. The delegates from the big cities – Dallas, Houston, and San Antonio – overwhelmed their rural colleagues with their preparation. I told my stories about getting the Rockwall Bank loan and the SBA 8(a) certifications to compete for large government contracts, large to me anyway. To the big companies led by white males, $100,000 was just a pittance. They worked in the upper atmosphere of millions of dollars, and these millionaires were fighting to keep smaller business issues off the platform. There were representatives from the chambers of commerce who spoke out against women and minorities as the enemy. They openly said all we wanted was a handout and that our issues would never make it to Washington.

My mission included two issues. First, I targeted eliminating the barriers for all women who wished to compete for government contracts or to get their share of business with large corporations. Second, banks needed to follow the laws relating to women, especially married women, while they concentrated on supporting all small businesses with loans and lines of credit.

During the two weekends of discussions about the state platform, I was excited to be a part of the talent that had gathered, but I was only successful in getting the bank loan legislation on the platform. I got to know well the delegates who supported the issues for women. We spent our free time together after the sessions at happy hour and dinner. When the sessions closed, off we went to the local hangouts where the state legislators drank after their work. We grabbed a table right next to the politicians who soon moved their chairs around our gathering. What a night it was. We gave out business cards and got the names of people to call in the legislative offices. Whether it was the liquor or the high-flying company, we were all filled with the hope that this could increase our business.

It was around these tables, as well as during the daily meetings, that I developed very deep and lasting friendships with the women and men representing Dallas. We planned our campaign, sometimes well into the night, to get our Dallas delegation leader, Dave Pinkus, elected to lead us all to Washington D.C. Along with Dave, Wanda Brice, Doris Thomas, and Valerie Freeman became very good friends.

Excitement filled the air in Washington as we struggled to support our platform in competition with all the other states. Delegates who had attended the previous 1980 White House Conference on Small Business under Jimmy Carter became the leaders of these sessions and seemed to have more power to support their platforms.

At most White House conferences, the President of the United States typically appears. But meeting with President Reagan at the White House was not on the agenda. In 1986, Reagan went on vacation during the conference. We knew that he deliberately snubbed us. He was against any form of affirmative action for women and minorities. We 8(a) contractors were afraid that Reagan would cut the legislation and the money that supported the program, so we united behind the SBA. The National Federation of Independent Businesses joined the United States Chamber of Commerce to back Reagan's goals, to eliminate the SBA.

At every meeting, we presented our case. Although a large percentage of small businesses, mostly rural, supported the President and his Republican party, we had enough supporters who were riled up. And we gathered enough delegates to defeat both Reagan and the white male giant organizations. We lost a few of our battles to the powerful white male cadre, but we safeguarded the future of the SBA and the loans that they administered to support us. The SBA was our chief lifeline to financial success. For us, the whole conference activity of the past six months was worth it.

Reagan promised to put women in top posts, but he had no women in his cabinet in 1986. Sandra Day O'Connor's appointment to the Supreme Court was his only meaningful action. We women delegates felt our support would have to come from Congress. It was there where we would get our bank laws to end discrimination.

This White House Conference experience was the beginning of my public and political advocacy for women-owned businesses. The local SBA, once my nemesis, valued my assistance at the conference and often requested I give keynote speeches at their small business conferences. I joined our local Dallas NAWBO group, and the stories in the next chapter will show the strength of women in networking. Although many women had been advocates for women before the conference, for me, the conference proved the stimulant to advocate specifically for women business owners.

CHAPTER TWENTY-SEVEN

The Fight for Women's Business Equality

IN ORDER TO GROW OUR ENTERPRISES, Dallas women entrepreneurs found that networking was essential to obtaining new business. We determined that, because of the preposterous strength of our white male competition, we would become members of the Dallas - Fort Worth Minority Supplier Development Council (D-FW MSDC). I know that sounds ironic. Why wouldn't we want to hook up with the powerful white guys? Simple, they didn't want us. But the Council was set up for the sole purpose of giving minorities and women opportunities to market their businesses.

The MSDC Board of Directors wanted us. The Defense Department and the SBA were pressing them to do business with minorities and females. Their intent was to show us the ropes about how to approach their companies for business. All of the people on the MSDC Board of Directors represented some of the largest public and private businesses in the Dallas - Fort Worth area.

Whether a business owner was Hispanic, African American, Asian, or female, we all had the same interests — to get a piece of the corporate and government procurement pie that universally fell to the white male business owner. The MSDC was a dynamic organization that was our only network to get larger contracts. Before the procurement officers formed the MSDC, women and minority businesses could not get a hearing in the procurement departments which were responsible for offering contract work. My multiple experiences with local companies proved this as did that of other women-owned businesses.

Since the Council had the major players in local corporate purchasing on its board and among its all-white male members, this was our chance to network with them at board meetings and "Meet and Greet" activities. We knew that all things being equal, landing business with corporations and even with government is dependent on who you know. The government contractors functioned as though this was not true, but we all knew the government was not unlike corporations. White males ran the departments.

We minority and women businesses were not a priority, and we were all unhappy that these corporations were not doing much purchasing from us. At the same time, a small cadre of minority owners thought the white women in the organization were the problem. They made moves to have white women removed from MSDC membership because they thought the pie was not big enough to be shared. They proclaimed that we were fronts for white males — specifically, we married women were accused of fronting for our husbands. The pie was hundreds of billions of dollars, and we wanted our share.

The local MSDC was affiliated with the National Minority Supplier Development Council out of New York City. That national body declared that women business owners may not be members of local councils. They could do that because the laws protecting women from discrimination did not apply to non-profit associations like the MSDC! This National Council's new rule targeted the D-FW MSDC because it was the only local council in the nation that had white women as members.

At first, the Board of Directors voted to ignore the national threat because they thought it was illegal and unjust. But this didn't last long. The Dallas minority owners had power with this national organization and with the local board. The national group threatened to withdraw financial support, which was 20% of the local council's budget. Money talks. The Board voted us out, so we waged a battle.

I was one of 95 women whom the board ejected as members of the MSDC. Together with five other women, I took the leadership role in confronting the MSDC Board. Three of these women represented powerful organizations of over 400 women: Doris Thomas, the Dallas NAWBO President; Jackie Statman, President of AWED; and Sherrie Hall, Women in Construction. Wanda Brice and Valerie Freeman had both held presidencies of women's groups and were equally passionate about attaining justice and success for women business owners, as were Susie Marshall, Billie Bryant, Bette Price, and Nicki Nicole.

J-DL was a national company with nine offices from Texas to the East Coast and 500 employees. Our business was fairly independent of what happened locally, except for the prime government contractors. I was in the fight for justice for women business owners. J-DL was committed to advancing the role of women in business and government. I had personal experience with the male chauvinism of the military-industrial complex and knew that this would be a hard fight. I had very little to lose, so I became Chair of the Women Business-Owners Task Force. Vivian Castleberry called us "Women Warriors" or "Wonder Women" in her book (*Seeds of Success: How a Few Women Changed the Landscape of American Business, 2006,* Womens Enterprise Magazine, p.10).

We met frequently with members of the page, especially with the chair, who was the Vice President of Procurement for Texas Instruments. At first he was very supportive of women retaining their membership and led the board to adopt a resolution that supported his view. The board told us that they did not see the need for voting us out, but the national group had tied their hands.

We also met with the minority members who opposed our membership. The negotiations with these members were open and direct, but difficult. Eventually, the board began to meet secretly and became less open to negotiating with us. Consequently, we felt pummeled on all sides. Our first alternative, beyond a lawsuit, was to raise the battle to the public.

PUBLICITY

The ejection of women from the MSDC membership did get public attention when the *Dallas Morning News* ran three stories in July 1992. On July 10, six of us women met with the chair, at his request, to hear that the board had voted to revoke "all non-minority memberships" from the MSDC. He told us that a press release from the board would appear in the paper the next morning. We immediately wrote our own press release and sent it to the paper, announcing that we were very happy to provide the paper with another perspective on this story from the women who had been ejected from MSDC. The two stories appeared the next morning. Our women's version hit the front page, and the board's appeared on an inside page.

A third article written by Bill Deener appeared on July 15, 1992. Mr. Deener had interviewed us at one of our meetings, and the paper published a photo of six of us. He interviewed most of us women as well as the MSDC Chair. The article was supportive of the women's cause and highlighted the injustice of this action. The story also related that a board member had received a frightening threat of violence. Making this threat public raised the anger level of all three constituents. The publicity did not turn the decision in our favor as we had hoped it would.

RAISING THE RISK LEVEL

Our next move was to take our cause to the highest levels of the corporations. After many brainstorming sessions, we decided to send a letter to the Chief Executive Officers of the 250 members of the national body, NMSDC. We personalized each letter with the CEO's name and sent it in the overnight mail to arrive on each of their desks the next morning.

We aired the history of our fight to remain in the MSDC after being expelled solely because we were white women. We described the burden that the National MSDC had demanded of the local MSDC, get rid of the white women, or we will withdraw our support and expel your organization from the National Council. We also told of threats that a board member reported to us. Finally, we requested that the CEO instruct his representative to acknowledge our membership and to support the organization.

As Castleberry wrote, quoting Wanda Brice, "All hell broke loose." Yes, we went for the jugular and got some response before noon.

The local board was seething. The chair wasted no time inviting Doris Thomas and me to have lunch at the posh Mansion Hotel with him and the vice chair, the procurement officer of PepsiCo. Neither Doris nor I had been at the Mansion before, and we were impressed. Pink tablecloths and flowers adorned the table while soft lights set a peaceful mood. But we had waited 30 minutes for them to arrive, and the delay raised our temperatures to match theirs. Red-faced, the chair started with "What were you thinking? We were handling this."

No apologies like, "I'm sorry, we were held up." No handshake. No greeting. Just like the proverbial bull in the china shop, he continued to humiliate and disrespect us. He and the vice chair had been embarrassed and humiliated by their bosses, so they took it out on us. They had expected us to accept the decision. That was not going to happen.

I spoke up. "No, you weren't handling it to our satisfaction. You sacrificed us, and we are not going to sit silent. You forced us to write that letter because you thought we would go quietly. Although the minority threats that we heard were menacing, we refused to be frightened by whatever they were. We are not even sure they were real."

"Yes, they were real," the chair said.

Finally, these two men produced a compromise. They suggested that the board would be open to supporting a second organization for women locally. This was an idea from the sky, something hatched in their morning chaos. They had no support for this scheme from the board as of that moment. There was no plan to gain this support, and likewise, no strategy for getting the financial backing for such an organization. This was candy offered to the female children. We knew that the corporations could have contributed sufficient funds to make up for the $60,000 or 20 percent of their budget that they would lose if they allowed the women to remain.

We left unsatisfied, telling them – if and when they could bring this to fruition with an organization equal to the present MSDC – we would consider it. We doubted that the corporations would be willing to support two organizations. This whole rejection of women happened because the corporations said they couldn't afford to lose the financial support of the national council. The minorities in New York and Washington D.C. were very powerful, and the minority members in Dallas - Fort Worth wanted a piece of that power. By separating from white women, they got their opportunity.

Throughout this battle, what ate at my soul the most was that our fellow minority members were calling us racists. If anything motivated me from my days in the convent, it was social justice and fighting racism, prejudice, and gender bias. Despite the fact that African American and Hispanic women had not been very successful in procuring business from these corporations, they did not choose to join the white women. This fight touched all of our souls. Of course, over the years, we have learned that white women have not supported black or brown women many times when they had the opportunity.

The women of color, also poorly treated by these white male representatives, would not abandon their men even though they told us that they understood our cause. It is true that we white women did not consider the history of racism in this country of ours, nor the feelings of the African Americans who saw us white women as simply white people of privilege. From their viewpoint, we were displacing them again by trying to join them in our common cause of growing our business in the light of justice. This was not true of all the minority members, but for those who led the fight to expel white women members, there was no doubt in their words.

In this cause, the Hispanic and the African American women joined forces against us. Some could not see through their lenses that white men had subjugated white women for centuries. We women could not see that the minority view was ingrained through centuries of slavery and abuse by whites, whether men or women. Women were simply chattel in Texas until 1965. We were fighting for our rights also. Neither we women nor the minorities saw the other's point of view. The procurement officers of the MSDC invited all of us into membership in the

MSDC as equals. And the white corporate males tried to avoid the suffering their companies might endure if this matter did not get settled.

With the offer of a separate Women's Council, I stepped back from the leadership role. Doris Thomas and Billie Bryant began the work with the vice president of Texas Utilities and a few other corporate representatives to build the council. I felt this would be a lengthy process, and I had already taken enough time away from my business to help restore women to the MSDC. The project was safe. The Texas Utilities procurement officer took over as chair of the local minority council. J-DL had done business with Texas Utilities, and I knew the company and its CEO, Earl Nye, would follow through on their offer to support the women.

The women continued to work to establish the North Texas Women's Business Council. The newspaper publicity had produced something good: it had raised women's hopes. The Dallas Citizens Council took action. They asked their corporate members to determine the numbers of women in management jobs and to report it to the Dallas Citizens Council. Vivian Castleberry's book relates that, in those three years after the expulsion of women, the Women's Council became a reality. Its mission was to certify the women business owners as women-owned businesses, to educate women about operating a business, and to assist corporate executives in working with women business owners.

Eventually our efforts with women-owned businesses in Dallas became the springboard for Gale Duff-Bloom, Executive Vice President of JC Penney, to form a national organization with the same responsibilities to certify women-owned businesses, to educate them, and to connect them with corporate supply chains. The Women's Business Enterprise National Council (WBENC) became a powerful force in supporting women to grow their businesses. Women-owned businesses became a very significant segment of our economy. I take pride in my contributions and those of other women in Dallas that all our efforts resulted in tens of thousands of women certified and operating successful businesses.

Most of all, I take pride that this movement was the catalyst for the establishment of SBA's Women Business Owners Federal Contracting Program. Women now have a program to compete for federal contracting. They no longer needed the SBA 8(a) program that I successfully sued to be a part of, the one that permitted J-DL to get off the ground and running.

CHAPTER TWENTY-EIGHT

And Now What?

SHOULD A WOMAN'S VOICE be silent when she retires?
In 1995, I sold J-DL. Life looped back to my inner need to reestablish touch with the God who had provided so well for me. My intention when I left the convent was to produce a life that would serve God's purpose. God, I believe, wants Her people to be happy and to help them to take control of their lives. I hoped my work had done that. But now that this work was finished, what should I do?

A year earlier, Robert and I had purchased some land on a ridge in Mt. Crested Butte, Colorado. The best description of living there was serenity. The perfect place for a writer in rural silence, created for meditation, deep thought, and prayer.

Robert and I loved Crested Butte, the spectacular beauty of the mountains, the dear friends we made, but life changed as the years passed. Robert had some eye issues triggered by living at an altitude of 10,000 feet, and I grew tired of eight months of snow and two months of mud season. We left Crested Butte for warmer weather in the desert of Southern California and bought a home in a new developing Del Webb Sun City.

This place was unusual. In addition to its being a development for people over 55, everyone came looking for a new life. The Del Webb concept offers opportunities for people to develop their individual interests. Robert and I chartered a Bridge Club with 20 other people as well as a Democratic Club. Robert was initially involved in the establishment of two clubs: a computer and a camera group. A group was also formed to develop a community magazine, and I was invited to do some stories for it. Excitement filled our lives as we met new people, developed friendships, and committed to new interests. We were impressed with the experience and talent of our neighbors who dedicated their time and skills to collaborate with others simply by volunteering.

Collaborating with others on the magazine, called *The View*, inspired me. After a year, I agreed to teach a memoir class for the Communications Committee so that we could attract more neighbors to write for the magazine. I had 15 new writers in that class. Out of it came not only writers for the magazine but dear friends.

Working with such creative colleagues required a monthly meeting I looked forward to. The group was filled with intellectual humor and produced a magazine of very high quality. We wrote about our surrounding neighborhoods, and we soon received humorous contributions from some fledgling authors. This literary production allowed us to search out stories that would help our senior community with health issues, inspiring stories for new retirees, profiles of our neighbors who had led interesting lives, and volunteer opportunities with charities. I feel my writing and my life has purpose.

Our committee members had excellent experiences on magazines. When I was in Dallas, I wrote a column on small business for the *Dallas Times Herald* as well as many articles for my J-DL clients. My dear friend and fellow editor, Lee Powell, had previously been a writer and editor for a federal government agency. Steve Talbot had experience as a writer and editor for a corporate magazine. Bill Singer was a writer and editor for corporate training publications. Beth Bolduc came from an Art Director's position on an artistic publication, and she and Arnold Choy were students in that memoir class I taught. Linda Assen, Dennis Sheehan, Julie Harris, Ralph Olson, Gina Pollack, and Bob Firring also brought their corporate writing and management skills to us.

Working with them is such a creative experience that you catch their passion, engage in their ever-flowing ideas for new articles, and are grateful for their willingness to be there with their support when you mess up. Catching up on community facts or rumors feeds our interests. We have a theme, "Writers need constant new material so rumors, stories, and even gossip are very welcome."

I have taken a sabbatical so I could complete these memoirs that have been underway for five years. When this book is on its way to publication, I hope to rejoin the committee. I miss it very much — the laughter, the creativity, and most of all the process of producing what we see as a literary magazine reflecting the richness and talents of our community.

My life here in the desert has enabled me to lead very full and joyful days. Yes, I am sure there are friends I have offended, colleagues that wish I would not let my voice be heard, and dear friends who wish they had never heard my language on the golf course. I suppose those days in the convent suppressed this voice, but now I can admit the voice has been heard.

I hope this book inspires other women to shout out when necessary, to speak politely when it would be more beneficial, and to be true to their natures as women with spirit.

Gratitude: Friends
Give Me Spirit in My Life

G ATHERING A SPIRIT OF EMOTIONAL SUPPORT and honesty, appreciating guaranteed laughter, and contemplating soul-searching questions that make me examine who I am – these things flow from my women friends.

The research that was done out of UCLA by Laura Cousins Klein, Ph.D. and Shelley Taylor, Ph.D. on why we women need our women friends "suggests that women respond to stress with a cascade of brain chemicals that cause us to make and maintain friendships with other women." Dr. Klein claims that,

> *"...when the hormone **oxytocin** is released as part of the stress responses in a woman, it encourages her to tend children and gather with other women. When she actually engages in this tending or befriending, studies suggest that more oxytocin is released, which further counters stress and produces a calming effect."*

Dr. Klein further states that this calming response does not occur in men because testosterone — which men produce in high levels when they're under stress — seems to reduce the effects of oxytocin while estrogen seems to enhance it.

The dearest friends follow you wherever you go. You learned about the wonderful women that befriended me at Notre Dame, and Mary Marg Dickinson has been in my life and that of my family for all of these years. *Principessa Una*, Pilar Raval, born in the Philippines, and I have been friends from our time in Dallas. How can one not love Pilar, with her cheerful personality, her love of life? If she were Irish, she would be the leprechaun with the pot of gold sprinkling it every step of the way for all following her path. Her joy is so contagious, I telephone to hear her laughter, to enliven my day.

Dianne Patterson, Wanda Brice, and I get together every couple of years for girl time. We were members of the International Women's Forum, and we frequently traveled to the annual conference together. Often we brought our husbands along to New York, London, Dublin, Israel, San Francisco, and Los Angeles.

Diane's talent as a business owner has been well recognized in Dallas, but her generosity and support for our friendship can never be honored sufficiently. My dear friend of 35 years springs to action when I am in need, calms my fears with her gentle words, loves and inspires me with her courage, and credits me with opening up her life to joy, when it is she who brings so much happiness to my life.

Wanda lost her husband, Tom, in 2020. We also lost Tom. Wanda has been by my side since 1986 when we were both delegates to the SBA White House Conference. We fought so many business battles together that our personal friendship bonded with well-deserved happy hours.

To Brenda Jackson, I give a shout-out. I do miss our breakfasts, our lunches, and our dinners. No, our friendship was not based on always eating. You are still in my heart. What would I and Texas Utilities (in all its names) have done without you? Elysia Ragusa, you may be in Austin now, but you will always be in my heart. Dolores and Larry Barzune, here's to your loving marriage and your friendship. And to those women friends who brought sustenance to my spirit through the Dallas Forum, thank you.

My time in Crested Butte carries so many dear friends who made my first retirement years exciting and joyful. Nancy Riemer gave me the honor of being her witness at her wedding to our lawyer-friend, Chuck Cliggett. Anita Puglisi made me laugh through her ever-present smile. She, Pam Jaynes, and Joyce Cavanaugh shared our books in our Red and White Book Club. Yes, the red and white signifies the importance of wine to our discussions.

When we moved to the Coachella Valley in the desert of Southern California, I found book clubs to be a great opportunity to meet women. At first I joined the Readers Ink Book Club at our new home in Shadow Hills. This association encouraged me to delve into books that I never would have read. Many of them were popular and bestsellers, but I just never seemed to catch up on familiar authors until I joined this 40-member book club. Eventually I yearned for something more intimate where the books could be discussed in depth.

My good friend, Merle Freedman, offered me the opportunity to join a group of simply brilliant women who called themselves the "Classic Chicks," and the classics were the book choices. I dearly love Merle, Nancy Angus, Connie Brennan, Renee Heller, Sue Kester, Mary Lee Niethold, and Sharon Warner.

Reading and writing are not my only interests here in the desert. Golf gets me outside each Friday with three of my dearest friends: Stacia Armstrong who has the eagle eye to spot all our balls, Pamela Castro-Lee who would drive us to play all day if we let her, and Charlene Harris who teaches all of us how to calmly enjoy our time together. We are women who practice being heard, and we love it. We play by the rules, adjusted for our friendship: one mulligan for each round, air swings don't count, and double the par on each hole is as high as you can score. When you are in the middle of each round, you cannot quit no matter how bad you are doing. I tried to quit once, and they just wouldn't let me give up. Then there is Donna Gambale who got us started in this golf game but did give up on golf. We miss you, Donna.

Among the four of us, we now count six marriages and 150 years of married life. So, we all believe we know something about marriage, or at least we talk as though we do. We all feel life is good, and if it's not, we know we need to do something about it. These dear women also share my religious values, our belief in God, in our Christianity, and in an afterlife. We are all strong volunteers in our SCSH community and feel duty-bound that, if you live here, you are obligated to make the community a valuable experience. Who wouldn't love us? I do. Each of these friends has an important place in my heart.

I met my dear friend, Jennifer Hendrix, at a Halloween party in October of our first year here at SCSH. She and her husband, Bill, have become our Sunday afternoon bridge players. Often we join with others, particularly Charles and Barbara Hite; bridge as well as close friendships are a combination that never fails for us.

I was having lunch with Jennifer Hendrix and Stacia Armstrong, and they were discussing a new group they had formed that I was unaware of. They recognized that I was in the dark about their conversation. (I did feel left out.) They explained that it was a group called Women of Color, mostly black and some Hispanic women. Jennifer said, "Would you be interested in being my guest at the next meeting? There's no reason why you can't join. Come and see what you think?" I was grateful to be invited. I was amazed at the warmth and acceptance of the group. All the women were residents of Sun City Shadow Hills. It was a great opportunity for me to get to know new people.

For a year, I was the only white woman in the group. At first, until I got to know the women, I was concerned about my presence. Did I belong to this group? Would I be an interloper? Yes, I was the outlier but only in the color of my skin. In all other ways, we had so much in common. They wanted me, and I wanted them. My upbringing and theirs were built on different cultures, but we treasured the same values: family, friendship, fashion, other women's fun topics, and Democratic politics. What else would we need to enjoy each other? I love these women and am so grateful to be accepted into their warm hearts.

I am forever grateful to Sid Weiss and his wife, Donna, for starting our movie discussion group and building this form of entertainment into an educational experience for us. And to Bara and Arnie Rosenheck for gathering us into your warm arms. Ray Fay and Ingrid, I am sorry you moved away. I miss you.

My husband, Robert, is my best friend. He strengthens my spirit with his humor and encouragement along each step of my journey, his generosity in equally sharing our family and household responsibilities, and most of all, how much he loves and cares for me.

These friendships, and all those who have slipped my memory, have enlivened my life, activated my brain, and cultivated a joy that I have not found in my years of working. Some people hesitate to retire, and I understand the hesitancy if "retire" means being bored, having no friends, or being a couch potato. But my friends here at Sun City Shadow Hills encourage active friendships. To them I am grateful. Even in retirement we must assure that we play our part to make life fulfilling. To be fulfilled is to participate, to contribute, and truly to be heard.

SPECIAL ACKNOWLEDGEMENT

Special gratitude goes to those who have supported me through this publication: Chris Molé has been my designer and continued source of support through the process of production, I am very grateful. Much gratitude also goes to Lee Powell, editor, for his support, and to Mark Malatesta and Howard Lovy for setting me on the right path. Bob Puglisi has been there through all of the many phases of this process, offering advice from his numerous publications of fiction and his latest memoir. For those readers who have helped make this a better read: James Armstrong, Stacia Armstrong, Arnold Choy, Ray Fay, Merle Freedman, Jamie McGrew, Pat Napoles, Dianne Patterson, Anita Puglisi, Lee Powell, Bara Rosenheck, Judith Sorensen, Dennis Sheehan, and Darlene Turner, thank you.

I hope you enjoyed your read. If you did, or if you didn't, please feel free to contact me at **info@aggiejordan.com**. I welcome your voice to be heard.

About the Author

AGGIE JORDAN is the former founder and CEO of Jordan-DeLaurenti, Inc, a training and contract management company. Since selling this business, writing has been her life's work. A former small business columnist for the *Dallas Times Herald* and *Prime Women*, an online magazine, and a writer for *The View*, the monthly magazine for the Sun City Shadow Hills Community in Indio, California. Aggie has produced over 60 articles for these publications. She is the author of *The Marriage Plan: How to Marry your Soul Mate in One year or Less*, and *The Book of Robert*, a biography of Robert DeLaurenti, a first-generation Italian immigrant. Aggie has enjoyed traveling with her husband to over 75 countries and is aiming for the 100 mark.

She has been a guest on many television shows, including the *CBS Morning Show* and *ABC Good Morning Dallas*, as well as a number of radio broadcasts. A native of West Pittston, Pennsylvania, a former nun, a teacher, and a relationship counselor, Aggie hopes to inspire women to have their voices heard whenever, wherever, and by whoever challenges their rights to human equality.

www.ingramcontent.com/pod-product-compliance
Lightning Source LLC
Chambersburg PA
CBHW060504130626
46553CB00002B/410